CREATIO EX SACRUM GEOMETRICA

Creatio Ex Sacrum Geometrica

THE MULTIDIMENSIONAL MIND AWAKENING

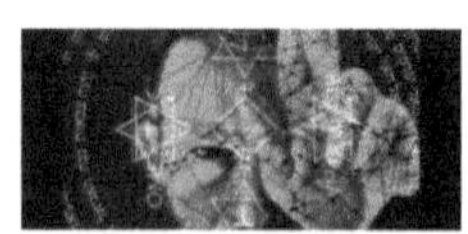

CREATIO EX SACRUM GEOMETRICA
THE MULTIDIMENSIONAL MIND AWAKENING

Quantum Consciousness, Divine light & the Alchemy of Metatron's Cube

The Pineal Portal

spiralling Into the deepest caverns of our being, housed within your temple we behold the grand alter that is the pineal gland. The centre point of our conscious existence. This sacred floral , pinecone-shaped gland has long been recognised across ancient cultures as the seat of the soul , in untold amounts of engravings and hieroglyphs its depicted being handed by the gods to man and now is widely believed and innerstood by those whom have been welcomed into the circle of the lost wisdoms to be representing the gift of divine consciousness and a gateway to realms beyond common perception.

When we explore our own consciousness, we find the pineal gland acts as a bridge between the conscious and subconscious realms. The day and the night and It is here, in this central sanctum, that the union of our waking reality and the infinite landscape of our dreams and intuition take place. This tiny gland represents the key that will unlock the full spectrum of human potential.

Prepare yourself as we deep dive from the edge of the pineal portal out into the vortex of time itself, we find ourselves emerge in a prehistoric age surrounded by primitive hunter gathers foraging nature for all of its offerings .Now contemplate the role of sacred plants flowers and fungi in propelling the evolution of consciousness. Picture again the distant past when our ancestors, the evolving apes, stumbled upon nature's medicines. In their quest for sustenance, they unknowingly ingested plants like sacred mushrooms, blowing the doors of perception wide open.

These entheogenic experiences, guided by the wisdom of the Earth, triggered profound shifts in cognition and perception, elevating the apes into beings capable of higher thought and introspection. The altered states induced by these sacred botanicals could have been the catalyst for the birth of Homo sapiens, sparking a cognitive revolution that rocketed us into the realm of self-awareness.

As consciousness expanded, so did the impulse to communicate these newfound insights.

Deep within dimly lit caves, our ancestors traced visions on stone walls, etching symbols and stories inspired by the kaleidoscopic landscapes of their enhanced minds. The images they created became a tangible expression of the sacred journey within , a testament to the convergence of the conscious and subconscious realms, as they began to project inner visions and imagination beyond themselves, manifesting !

Given that this was the case, it would go to stand that our ancestors would never have stopped taking these medicines and over hundreds of thousands of years if not millions they would have evolved to become beings of such intelligence, wielding and manipulating the universal laws within the parameters of all that's possible. These skills and powers could have led to the civilization that was responsible for the creation of the great pyramid itself. Its geometric alignment with every measurement of earth and its position to the sun, with its true purpose still unbeknown to us is shrouded in mystery. All we know is somewhere between there and here, common knowledge of its true purpose was lost but the DNA inside of us goes all the way back to the beginning so it's here we must look for answers.

<u>**AS WITHIN SO WITHOUT**</u>

In the journey of our evolution, the vibration of our verbalised emotions slowly metamorphosed into the harmonious cadence of language. The whispers of the pineal portal echoed through the corridors of time, shaping the very fabric of our linguistic tapestry. The eventual form of language manifested in a triadic process: 1. emotion/energy, 2. symbolism/visualization, 3. speech/communication. Interestingly, the number three holds profound significance in magick; sacred trinities appear throughout history, religion, and mythical tales—Adam, Eve, and the serpent, to name one. The number three, symbolised by the triangle, represents creation, form, and birth. Thus, from the communion with sacred plants, the symphony of human expression was born.

Sitting here regarding this ancient tale, we can ponder the profound interplay between the pineal gland, sacred plants, and the emergence of human consciousness. When these mind-blowing realisations come to your awareness, the past becomes the present, and the present can forge the future when embraced and acknowledged for the true nature of its essence. For we are already now sailing together in this exploration of the internal universe, where the echoes of our ancestral odyssey swirl. The pineal portal beckons us to unravel the secrets encoded in the very core of our being.

Navigating the vast expanse of thoughts, I found myself at the crossroads of uncharted truth. Initiating this journey feels like standing on the brink of the infinite universe, a realm at first glance appearing to be devoid of beginnings or boundaries, much like the cosmic canvas that lies above our heads in the night sky that some of us attempt to make sense of each day.

In our waking reality, we establish markers and constructs to navigate the seemingly limitless universe around us. We use red, the lowest vibrational colour, as a warning sign, and green, which represents the heart, to go. We have exits and entrances to establish order from the chaos. We have created gravity to explain what we experience in our waking daily reality. These markers, crafted by us, are tools of comprehension in the face of the unfathomable. However, as we transition into the dream domain, the very foundations of these constructs begin to crumble.

In dreams, my good friend, we can fly; we can be anything we choose once mastered. Within the enigmatic landscapes of our dreams lies the revelation of an unparalleled truth—the essence of our multidimensional mirror existence. It's in this realm that the lines between reality and imagination appear to blur, offering glimpses into a reality unbounded by the markers we so diligently place in our waking hours. As we traverse this landscape, the boundaries that structure our physical reality dissolve, and the kaleidoscope of our true existence unfolds.

<u>METATRON</u>

Metatron, the Angel of the Veil, once walked the Earth as Enoch before God transformed him into an Archangel. In ancient texts, he is said to have created a means to communicate with the higher self—a state of consciousness that may well be akin to God himself. It is the place where all is known, as thy know is all. Perhaps I can best describe this as the end of the rainbow: if you look for it externally, it will elude you. But we can go there now. Just close your eyes and join me. What you see will be a reflection of your inner self or what you have asked to see—messages, abundance, or the dream of a place we once stood and admired our pot of gold. Fear or happiness in the mind is a reflection of the vibration you hold within.

To change your vibration, we should remember the three-stage process of our ancestors: first, we must feel the emotion; in recognizing that, we can visualise it; and then we can communicate it. This doesn't mean shouting at someone and passing on your low vibrational energy. It means that communication is key to evolution. A problem shared is a problem halved. Don't you feel better now you've got that off your chest? Even writing on a piece of paper and throwing it into the fire or kneeling by your bed with your hands together in prayer, talking internally to your higher self, God, or Source. After all, long before the Bible, the placing together of your two hands and entering into a transcendental state would open up a portal to the higher self/vibration, whereupon your words and thoughts can be received by the universe and recognized as desires or communication to understand your path.

Archangel Metatron has reached out to me many times throughout my life, both through dreams and in waking consciousness. I once slept with a blue tourmaline crystal on my forehead—as you do! At that stage in my life, I wouldn't have said I was that spiritual, but clearly, even then, I was living in a way that most wouldn't. I was about 24, and it was 10 years after my initial consciousness explosion, and I was in a mental place where I had begun to see my abrupt awakening as less of a disaster or problem and more of a gift. Being incredibly inquisitive, thirsty for wisdom, and with greater passion for creativity and control over my path and destiny.

One morning, I had a dream where a being of the subconscious realm showed me the lottery numbers. I awoke remembering three of those numbers. I immediately went and placed lines that encompassed these numbers. I told a group of friends about this occurrence, and it was met with laughter and mockery, but also a sense of the inquisitive kind. As my friends knew I'd predicted things before on other occasions, it wasn't without merit that I should have announced this. In reality, looking back, my previous predictions were all down to observing patterns in sports and other things and recognizing the repetition of events. So what to some may appear as extraordinary senses at that time was really just a heightened sense of awareness of my surroundings and a mind that was observing and deducting in a mathematical manner. Which, in turn, many say is the foundation of what divine magick really is. In Aztec times, the high priest would claim knowledge of the gods by predicting the solar eclipse from understanding the celestial patterns, and keeping this knowledge for his higher gains made him revered and feared by the unknowing masses. So it seems, that was once regarded as a very high form of magick, but that is just the beginning of the insight we will uncover, completely lifting the veil on the journey of the seer to this point in time.

Going back to the lottery draw! The first ball that dropped, I had it. Everyone laughed. The second ball that dropped, I had. Everyone sat up. The third ball that dropped, I had. Everyone said, "What, no way!" Then no more balls matched my selections. Everyone said, "Well, that was mad." It was a very powerful moment, much more powerful than I even knew at the time. Zipping forward one year, I had moved house, and I got a phone call out of the blue from someone I had hardly ever really spoken to—a very random text saying, "Your Archangel is Metatron. The day you dreamed those lottery numbers wasn't so you could win the lottery. It was so you would believe there's more." It connected me to my higher self, to Archangel Metatron, to a force within the infinite.

I had a dream where I was shown many things, one of which was seeing Metatron's Cube close to me and watching it shift through all of the Platonic solids that it bears within its mathematical structure. Then it slowly moved away, revealing to me its pixelated place side by side with infinite copies of itself, morphing in its projected state, forming the dream synopsis we see with our mind's eye. I was in awe of this display, and it again was something that would never leave my consciousness. It was another level of initiation into the inner workings of creation.

The patterns we see in nature and life are here to guide us. Just like a clairvoyant can read tea leaves or tarot cards, everything in the visible domain you encompass will hold keys to higher paths. The more you read and trust this process, the more they reveal themselves to you. Guiding me when I've needed and showing me divine truths of the universe throughout the cosmic dance of patterns that weave the fabric of reality. From the intimate internal details to the colossal galactic formations, there exists this profound symbol of Metatron's Cube. Within its intricate geometry, we also find the blueprint of the atom, a microscopic dance of particles, as well as the majestic symmetry of a distant star. This sacred emblem becomes a portal to explore the realms of fractals and will lead us to the possibility and higher wisdom of an infinite fractal reality where demons, entities, gods, souls, and beings exist on vibrational, multidimensional tiers, where the microcosm and macrocosm converge.

Let me take you on a journey to unravel the tapestry of existence. Metatron's Cube serves as the very pixels that form the fabric of our inner sight and governs space in the physical domain. Where it leads us is a cosmic odyssey where numbers become a language, and the universe unfolds its secrets in the magick of sacred geometry.

A footnote

Verses in this tome shall unveil manifold meanings, akin to the Flower of Life. The central, sacred circle entwined with six, her sentinels. Those six, in turn, are enveloped by another six, weaving a cosmic lattice of divine geometry. As your thoughts meander through the labyrinth of perception, and as your emotions ebb and flow with the tides of your soul, the meanings you ascribe to these verses will transform. They are a mirror to your inner universe, a reflection of your emotional liberty and spiritual awakening.

<u>AWAKENING</u>

My love affair with Metatron's Cube began before I even knew consciously of its existence. I was seduced unknowingly by its energy from a very young age, enchanted by the excitement of creation, that infinite and never-ending genius of our imagination. Long before I knew or understood the mathematical brilliance of Metatron's Cube and the domain it represents within the universe, I was fascinated by musing and our affinity to dream. The human consciousness will bloom, and your insights, dreams, and visions are a testament to your connection with Metatron's Cube and the source light produced from the centre point of its multidimensional design.

As a child, I was so connected to my inner world, yet at the same time, a complete extrovert. I wasn't withdrawn, but my imagination would run wild, and I would allow it. I would play with it. I would embrace it. It would caress me, and I would caress her as I grew. My inner world was a sanctum, and I grew to understand my consciousness very quickly, but in doing so, I opened her up abruptly. To a breaking point, a fracturing of myself. I overnight became the observer of my own mind and not the puppet and actor of it. It was incredibly liberating and at the same time crippling and extremely scary! This was a Kundalini awakening induced by working through levels of social and internal programming in higher vibrational states until I burst through the veil, consciously and energetically. The immediate effect was I developed a host of, at that time, very unwelcome tendencies for a teenager. They were unwelcome then but entirely necessary for the ascension of consciousness from peripherally contained to celestially connected and able to exist as a being in the quantum realm. That is where a man is broken and dissipated or forged like a diamond under the pressure of infinity. At the same time, as a paradox once understood, you are free as a bird.

As it turned out, the tendencies I developed were all low, vibrational, fear-related hurdles I had to find a way to overcome upon the climb to the zenith of my mind. Whether they were past life echoes stored within my DNA, karmic debt, experiences of other versions of me from infinite dimensions, or just the figment of my imagination (lol), or what modern (lol again) distorted medical disinformationist would phrase as psychotic tendencies, PTSD, or anxieties. They were energies I had been abruptly introduced to and had to understand and form an alliance with.

Below is a large diagram of Metatron's Cube. I want you to take a moment to stare into it and allow it to show you its deeper dimensions. See if you can get a feel for its properties and ability to shift its form! You will see in the other pictures how its formation and design are apparent in the light reflecting from a star, in the basic composition of an atom, and in the sacred emblem of the Star of David. In this case, the hexagram (Star of David) is housed within a hexagon, forming the shape of an octahedron! This is very significant, and we will be coming back to this later when the moment is right.

- Metatron's cube Note how, in the broadest structure of Metatron's Cube, there is a cube shape formed from the perimeter of the hexagon by joining the six corners with internal straight lines. This sacred geometry conjures a profound and mystic vision, creating a six-dimensional axis emanating from the center point. Herein lies the secret of creation, the divine alignment, and the axis mundi connecting the heavens and the earth, the inner and the outer, the known and the unknown.

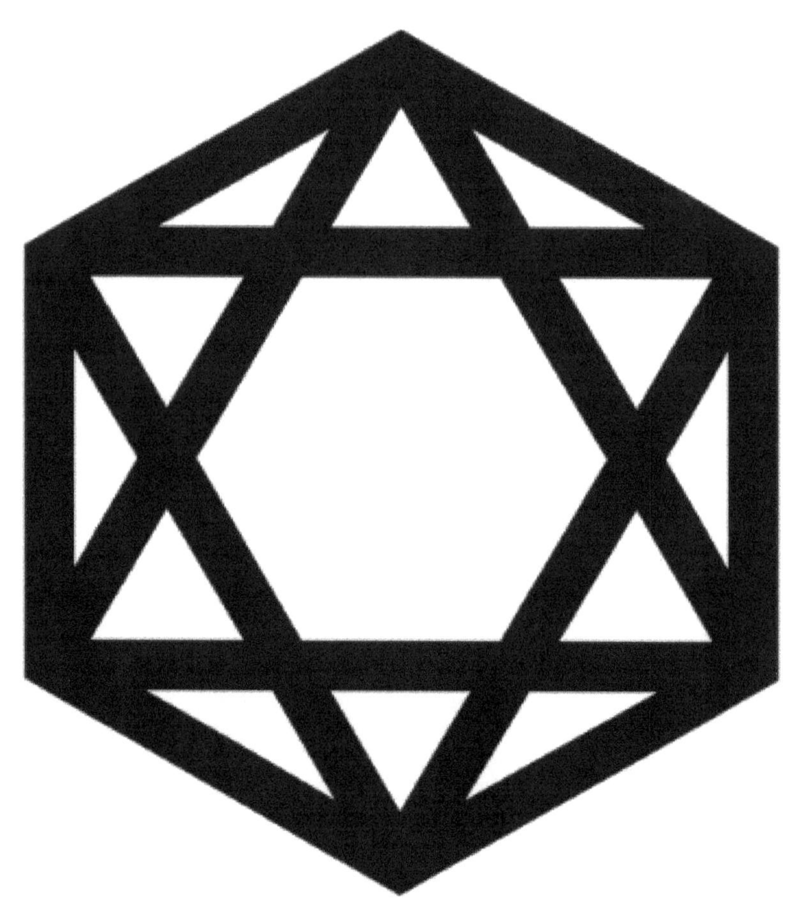

* Light of a star refracting

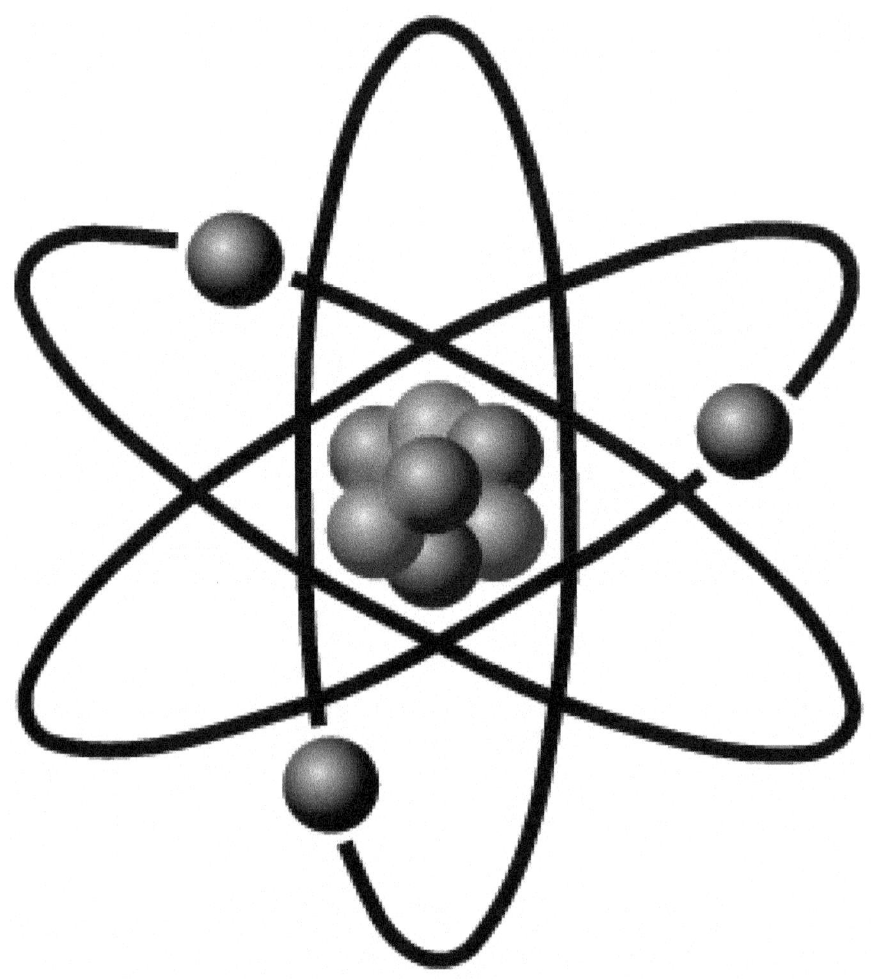

THE HIDDEN SACRED TRUTH OF THE MAGI CONSCIOUSNESS
Magic, in principle—Carl Jung said in the Red Book that the key to understanding magic lay within the hallucinations experienced in one's own mind. Whether through dreams, meditation, or enhancing vibrations with sacred medicines, let us take this a step further. Undoubtedly, understanding your hallucinations will increase your ability to perform, to call out to the universe, and to execute magical acts tenfold. This increases knowledge of what it is you're actually doing, for varying degrees of use. It is a tool to enhance your connection to divine truth, aligning with the sa-

cred geometrical reality built from the language of the universe. By connecting to your hallucinations, by seeing with your mind's eye, within your structure, you create your connection to everything, tracing a path through the connected universe (macro/micro, micro/macro).

You can call a cloud to move back, change the waves of the ocean, cause a plant to grow by calling in the force from the planets above, or summon visitors to your shop by creating a swirl in the minds of those seduced by your stock. When these thoughts (please have haste with your faults) are put into words and spoken aloud, they become even stronger. Just envision and see these connections; you will get results. For the fractional universe is all connected. One hexagon of Metatron's Cube is connected to the next, and when zooming in, you find the many. Zoom out, and the many become a few, like the hexagons of the honeycomb in the hive where each bee is connected to all, creating the nest—the core essence of magic.

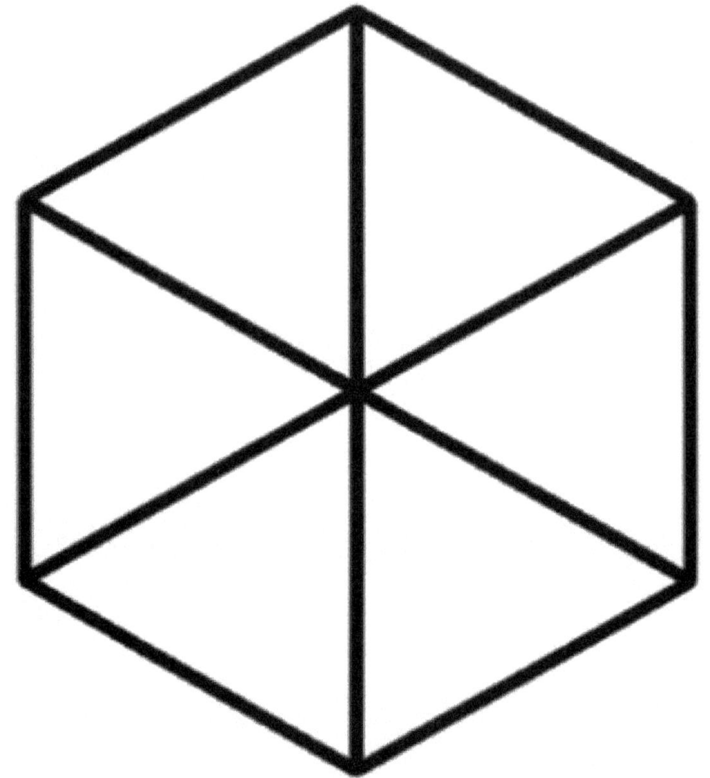

The above 3D cube manifests from 6 equilateral triangles. Adjacent to it, the 6-dimensional axis, the foundation of Metatron's Cube, unfolds before your eyes. Understanding this dimensional perspective grants insight into its profound significance. Initially perceived as basic elements, they unravel their hidden depths.

Below, the hexagram within Metatron's Cube gleams prominently. Composed of two equilateral triangles—one ascending, the other inverted—it bears the sacred symbols of earth, air, fire, and water, with ether at its core. This emblematic configuration resonates deeply within the cosmic order, revealing the interconnected tapestry of existence.

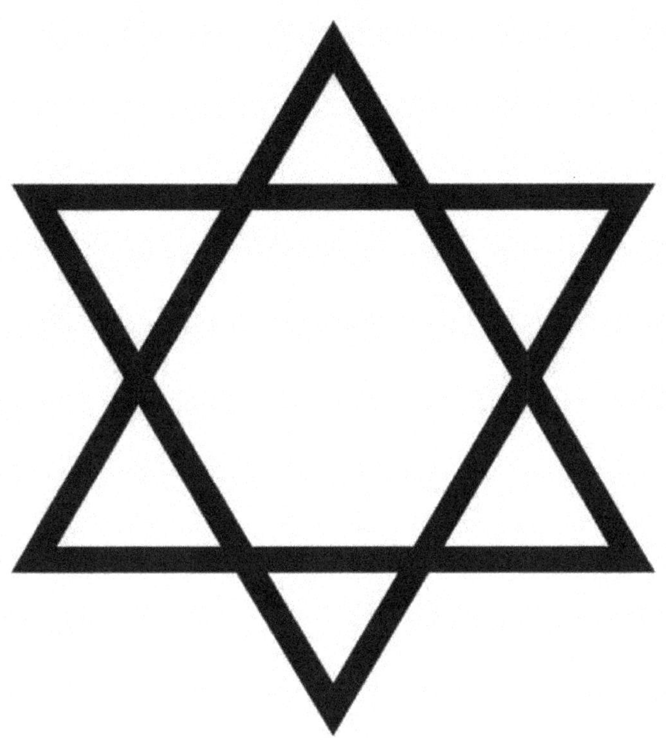

THE ETHER

I will briefly explain that the Ether is also known as the River of Souls to some and the Astral Light to ancient scholars. I will delve into this in much greater detail later, but to offer you a swift glimpse: it is the heart of the atom, the essence of the star. It resides as the seventh and central point at the Godhead of the hexagram, where black holes converge and matter dissolves into the infinite, where all things converge! A term that resonates with me is the Quantum Realm. Some refer to this as the Akashic Records. It is what Nikola Tesla, Leonardo da Vinci, Einstein—all the great minds of history—have attested to connecting with! Beyond themselves lies the vast unknown, where all things come to fruition! To exist in the vast unknown is to transcend material death! However, you must shed the inner box and be reborn into this boundless reality or be shown the path. The path cannot be seen until it is understood, either through a natural initiation or through teaching, and that is what I intend to convey in these texts. This divine understanding of the universe opens the mind to the science behind manifesting and sacred magic, the blueprints of our universe and our being.

<u>MULTIDIMENSIONAL MEANINGS</u>

The Great Pyramid stands sentinel, a lifeline akin to the placenta of humanity, reaching towards Orion's Belt—a mirror to the stars. The visible light or cord, under veiled conditions, emanating from its apex, anchors the ebb and flow of souls, holding the elusive key to our planet's evolution! It unravels why our consciousness, when delved into deeply, unfurls as a mathematical tapestry—the genetic coding of our energy and spirit upon delivery. These chains bind us, strings that magicians deftly pull.

The Journey - Cast off the fear of death and all that stagnates your passage along the path of experience. The unknown cannot be wielded if it controls; one must thrive within it, embrace it, accept its dominion, surrender to its fate, direction, and destiny. Through inner attainment, the zenith of potential unfolds—not for conquest, but for creation, to meet the genius within. When the fire ignites with the higher self of the mighty You, becoming part of the Almighty Plan, I convey this not as mere words, but as a truth long known.

The Inner Kingdom - Realms concealed, shrouded in mystery, beckon to be embraced, explored, and comprehended. When rooted firmly in the physical realm, fear of the unknown veils the profound truths of the universe. Uncover the sacred geometry, pause to delve into the creation within your mind itself. Distraction from delving into the depths of reality is akin to viewing a tree and savouring its fruit without pondering its hidden mechanisms and purpose.

The alchemy of carbon dioxide transmuting to life-sustaining oxygen underscores its sanctity. Ignoring its harmonies is the folly of closed hearts and foolish minds. Even within the labyrinthine workings of a tree, layers await exploration—what binds the tree to us, to the volcanic mountain's symphony in tandem with the springtime bloom? What unites the salmon's upstream journey and the scattered shells along a distant shore, all tethered within reach through Geometria's arcane weave from 1 to 9—it forms the intricate design.

<u>369 VIBRATION</u>

The magic of 369 is the answer to all of life's mysteries. A numerological riddle that was the life's work of so many priests, new-age thinkers, scholars, scientists, sorcerers, students, and masters—and if it wasn't, it surely should've been. Where to begin? The end is as good a place as any when discussing infinity, as that's what we are dealing with: the infinite universe and the infinite mind. The infinite universe without and within the mind—as within, so without. There is a clue that very old ancestors left us, a clue so incredible. It's so simple—it would live there for generations, recognized for its true meaning, yet marvelled at for its immense scale and physics-defying structural qualities. The architects of this great enigma were more than just ancestors. Perhaps they come from the stars and placed it here for guidance and as a symbol of the very fabric of consciousness and reality. The monolith I am referring to is the grand pyramids of Giza and its counterparts, its little brother and sister pyramids, the triad pyramid structures, and their three smaller ones , offsprings.

The pyramids' standing formation is exactly in alignment with the three stars that make up Orion's belt: Alnitak, Alnilam, and Mintaka. Perhaps this is an indication of where these beings came from, and they were built to convey it, like an artist signing their work. One thing about the great pyramid is that wherever you stand and look at it, you will see a triangle—you will see a three-sided shape, the only shape that can be made with three sides: a triangle. It is the smallest shape possible to create—as a two-sided shape would be void of form, non-existent. Triangle gives birth to form; it gives birth to creation. So, from a viewpoint of the ground, you will see an equilateral triangle—it is structurally elevated to allow the monolith to stand tall and to be observed. Remember I spoke earlier of how the hexagram has 6 points and a 7th central point ? Well this is presented to us in the structure of the pyramid with the triangle having 3 sides being housed on a square base with 4 sides ie 3+4=7 .

Let us explore the dimensions of the equilateral triangle. There are 3 of the inner corners that are 60° high. Independently 6+0=6 . If you then add those 3 corners together, 6+6+6—it creates 18, and 1 + 8 is nine, hence 369. As this Grimoire unfolds its content, it will unfold your mind. So all go in the knowledge—it contains to be understood, visualised, and used. You will become the knowledge that you seek, as it is also seeking you. I am you and the universe is—all of our parents our creator, and its truth is for all of us to be heard. Now, let's take into consideration the fact there are six pyramids. When you put six pyramids / equilateral triangles together, you get a hexagon, a two-sided two-dimensional shape that is made up of six equal actual triangles. If you change your perspective, it then becomes a 3-D cube. Look at the diagrams for a moment and let your perspective slide between the 2-D and 3-D shape. Let me draw your attention onto the secrets that lie within this template. Let me pull you in with the explanations as to why the symbol is so important and why its very nature is the key to the unlocking of the multidimensional mind. Show yourself to us so creatively, for we are ready to receive your wisdom.

The Microcosm—we are told that all matter is made up of atoms. Adam and Eve—the atom consists of the nucleus, surrounded by the electron of one or more electrons. At its most basic, we see this and by adding more electrons or dimensions within the structure increases , these are the building blocks of every element within the periodic table. Look into the diagram. I want you to assess the dimensional structure. This really is six dimensions in basic form , and is replicated from macrocosm to the microcosm. The microcosm—when you look into space into the night sky, you see the lights of the stars, shining back at you as they appear at an especially bright one. Do you see its rays , emanate and enter into your pupil, your black holes. The contours of light that no light escapes from. Your pupil receives,

Light is transmitted in your visual cortex and encoded instantly and made sense of by your brain into an image. Note this also with fire, and the ability to create false light our ability to illuminate ,akin to the light of the Sun.

"What is this light? Rays rebound from surfaces, penetrating your pupil. A dance of positive and negative, the Sun, in its masculine aspect, emits light and truth, engendering vision and revelation."

As stars age, they undergo a profound transformation, collapsing inward to form black holes that draw in everything around them. This process mirrors the intricate dance of creation and destruction seen throughout the cosmos. Light, in its simplest form, plays a dual role — emitting energy outward while also being drawn inward by gravity.

On Earth, we often perceive masculine and feminine energies as separate and distinct. In contrast, the celestial realm reveals their unity, seamlessly transitioning between creative and transformative forces. Here, destruction is not a fearful end but a vital part of an eternal cycle that sustains existence.

When we gaze into space, we peer into the very fabric of reality itself, woven intricately by our inner vision. Yet, our earthly existence is often dominated by figures of authority — leaders, politicians, and corporate giants — who dictate societal norms. They are flanked by pharmaceutical companies focused more on profit than on our well-being, and energy corporations driven by financial gain.

However, amidst this complexity, the 1960s brought a profound awakening. Visionary artists of the psychedelic era created cultural catalysts that expand our consciousness and reshape our reality. Their legacy continues today as a wave of activists courageously promote and distribute healing , challenging outdated norms and sparking global change.

Substances such as MDMA and magic mushrooms have been researched in safe, controlled environments and are well documented to offer profound healing and insights, fostering empathy, resolving inner turmoil, and strengthening neural pathways in the brain. Cannabis, a natural remedy, provides relaxation and pain relief while forging deeper connections within ourselves.Yet, amid this journey of self-discovery and societal evolution, we must remain mindful of the darker influences. Alcohol, in its excess, dulls our spiritual awareness and inhibits our growth.

Ultimately, our words and beliefs shape our reality. By aligning our inner truths with the universal rhythms of creation and transformation, we participate in a collective awakening that transcends individual experience. This journey invites us to embrace change, cultivate empathy, and forge connections that nourish our souls and propel humanity toward a brighter future.

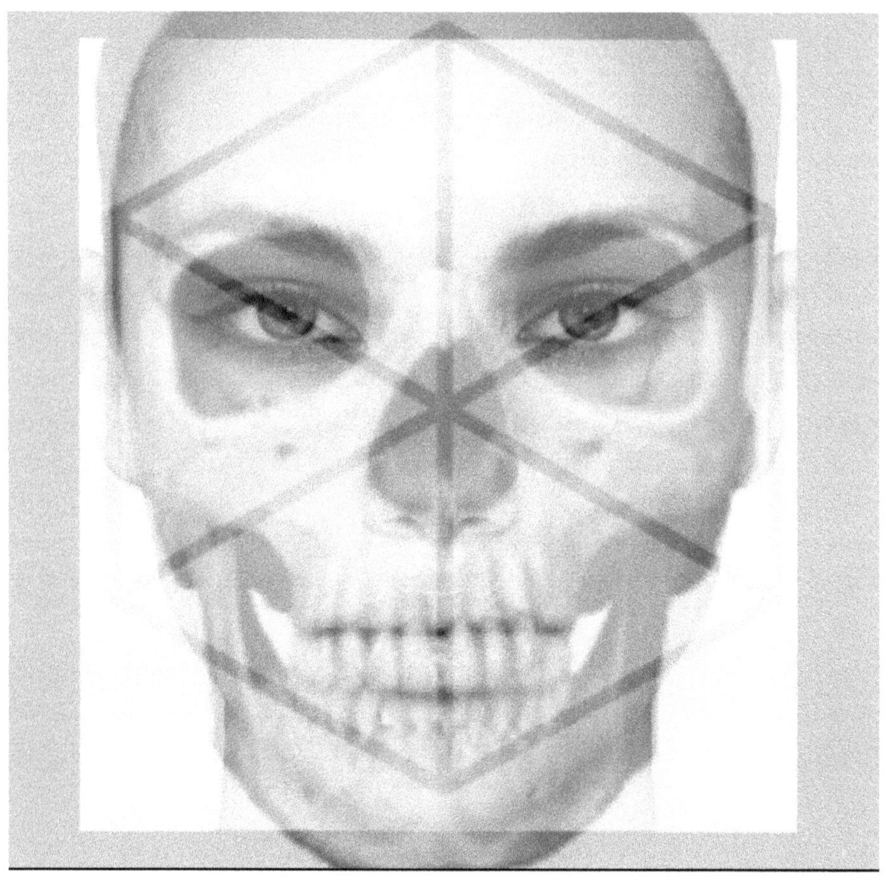

MKUltra, the mind's eraser, reveals your existence, ensnared within the confines of the TV's hypnotic spell, entwined deeply with intentional influence, and integrated with the channels of emotional feeling. I command you to erase, unplug, delete, and then meticulously reprogram your language—both to others and to yourself. View and observe your words keenly, for they possess a potent vibration that resonates through the fabric of your being. They fuel the internal belief systems that shape your reality. Depending on what lies within your deepest chambers, negative or positive, your words will inexorably reinforce. Thus, the alchemy of perception and belief transforms the very essence of existence itself.

"The fire kindles a light, its ashes fading from sight. The elements dance free —thus begins the magic within you and me. Some call it paranoia, others clairvoyance, and yet more of higher guidance—each facet dwells within, reflections of myself in you. Some deem it superstition, others intuition, a few discern the apparitions—all dwell within, a mosaic of the hidden realms within you."

THE INFINITE CONTINUAL REALITY

TRANSMISSION RECEIVED : ....

...... Welcome to The Multidimensional Mind Awakening ....

Origin : The Infinite reality

Objective : Freedom ....internal / external Growth .... expansion of awareness .... Health through true higher vibrational consciousness

I AM my teacher I AM my guide I AM my messiah I AM meditative I AM vibration I AM energy I AM tantric I AM chakras I AM infinite I AM healing I AM crystaline I AM Akashic records I AM source I AM love I AM ALL !

All come from the infinite space , the quantum realm , the origin of all creation .

Light serves the dark to create balance and ascending shifts of consciousness !

Open your chakras , fill them with the light of love, for everything is real , every dream and thought you feel .

"I can fold myself away into the smallest of details and find infinity or unfold myself from the tiny sparkle of the furthest star in the night sky to create an eternal expanse so vast , filled with unlimited creation !"

ANCIENT WISDOM

In the journey of ascent, from darkness into light, one emerges untethered, liberated from the Halls of Amenti, adorned with the Flower of Light and Life.

Guided by the luminous streams of wisdom and knowledge, he transcends mortal confines to reach the Master of Life.

Within the radiant flower, he communes with the Masters, released from the shackles of night's obscurity.

Enthroned amid the brilliance, seven Lords from transcendent Space-Times preside, shepherding humanity through the boundless arc of time.

Mysterious and potent, veiled in their sovereignty, they draw the currents of life, distinct yet united with mankind.

Distinct, yet One with the Children of Light.

Guardians and sentinels of humanity's bondage, poised to release upon the attainment of illumination.

Foremost and august, veiled in omnipresence, the Lord of Lords, the infinite Nine, presides over the others, each Lord of the Cycles: Three, Four, Five, Six, Seven, Eight, each with purpose, each with dominion, guiding the course and fate of man.

There they abide, mighty and sovereign, liberated from the constraints of time and space.

"YOU ARE THAT VAST THING THAT YOU SEE FAR , FAR OFF WITH GREAT TELESCOPES "

"If thou but settest foot on this path, thou shalt see it everywhere." "The excellence of the soul is understanding; for the man who understands is conscious, devoted, and already godlike." "No eyes will raise to heaven. The pure will be thought insane and the impure will be honoured as wise.

REROUTING THE CONSCIOUS TIMELINE TO THE OPTIMAL DIMENSION THROUGH WILL, INTUITION, UNDERSTANDING, UNITY AND MANIFESTATION

SEEK AND YE SHALL FIND

The Fibonacci sequence, a mesmerising pattern found in the heart of nature and mathematics, reveals a profound truth about the nature of existence. Each number in the sequence is the sum of the two preceding ones, creating an ever-expanding spiral that reflects growth and harmony. This sequence is not merely a path of outward expansion; it is also a journey inward, a return to the source. As we follow the Fibonacci path, we discover that the outward quest for knowledge and the inward search for understanding are one and the same. The journey outward leads us to the universe's vastness, while the journey inward brings us to the core of our being. In this fascinating dance of numbers, we find that the path both in and out converge, an interdimensional gateway allowing for travel or communication between different realms or levels of existence.

The Shamanic Experience

The first encounter with a shaman was a revelation—an energetic, healing journey that beckoned me to speak freely in ways previously unexplored. At first, I questioned its efficacy, dismissing it as mere placebo or gimmickry. Yet, upon reflection, a profound truth emerged: the mind's belief shapes our reality. Through the shamanic lesson, I learned the power of intention and belief in shaping our experiences.

Guided by the shaman's wisdom, I delved into introspection, probing the depths of my desires and inquiries. Setting intentions became a potent practice, leading to profound revelations and synchronicities. In dreams and altered states, I encountered symbols and emotions that unraveled the mysteries of my psyche, offering insights into my fears, desires, and the interconnectedness of all things.

A pivotal moment arrived during a psilocybin journey, unearthing the eternal beauty and boundless energy of the universe. Confronting my fear of death, I traversed the landscapes of memory and emotion, undertaking shadow work to heal the wounds of my past. The shaman's teachings resonated within me, guiding me through the labyrinth of my psyche toward wholeness.

Years later, a salvia experience shattered my perceptions once more, revealing hidden truths and ancestral echoes. In the depths of unconsciousness, I glimpsed the machinations of history—the legacy of MK Ultra and the enigma of Frank Olson. The revelation of past lives intertwined with mysticism and the occult, illuminating my path with newfound clarity.

Through research and introspection, I uncovered the threads that bound me to Nikola Tesla and his esoteric knowledge. The pentagram, the hexagram, the pyramid—symbols of universal vibration and hidden truths. Each revelation deepened my connection to a past steeped in mystery and influence.

In the tapestry of my life, psychedelics emerged as catalysts for transformation and revelation. Frank Olson's legacy cast a long shadow, guiding me toward the edges of consciousness and beyond. Though fraught with peril, the journey into the depths of the mind was an odyssey of self-discovery—an initiation into the mysteries of existence

Many Gifts Will Be Bestowed upon the believer , leaps of faith will take us on a journey that would otherwise lay undiscovered and the offerings never go unseen or unrepaid . We reap what we sow , as the will to receive begins with an outward flow .

Everything moves by the power of the soul , we are multidimensional beings within the cosmos of the creator .The multidimensional path to unity with the divine immortal mind .

In the mystical annals of occult, psychic, metaphysical, mystical, and esoteric lore, it is proclaimed that manifold planes of consciousness unfurl across the cosmic expanse. These esoteric doctrines, though draped in varying veils of terminology by diverse schools of mystical thought, intertwine and intermingle in a web of profound dimensions — spanning the ethereal domains of "physical," "mental," "spiritual," and "transcendent."

At the genesis of this cosmological tapestry lies the physical plane — the palpable realm of the material universe, governed by the sacred symphony of space, time, energy, and substance. Revered in the secret teachings of Neoplatonism, Hermeticism, Hinduism, and Theosophy, this plane stands as the bedrock, the densest manifestation within the celestial hierarchy. According to the sacred precepts of Theosophy, beyond the corporeal plane lies the etheric realm, inseparably intertwined to form the inaugural (physical) plane. Here, upon the mortal coil's unwinding, the etheric vessel endures, as the soul ascends to inhabit an astral form within the luminous precincts of the astral plane.

Beyond these corporeal spheres, lies a world of spectral images, shimmering in the metetherial dream-realm. In this ethereal domain, apparitions assume tangible form, transcending the boundaries of mundane reality to weave their spectral dance.

Thus, within the enigmatic folds of arcane knowledge, these planes of existence unfold as enigmatic layers, beckoning the seeker to unveil the mysteries of existence and traverse the astral currents that shape our spiritual voyage through the vast and mystic cosmos.

While modern day science used to look at DNA as a material object that was fixed in nature, therefore unable to be changed, where we were at the "mercy of our genes" so to speak, we now know that this isn't true. DNA is actually composed of a liquid crystalline substance that acts as a form of antenna, receiver, and transmitter of holographic information. It's constantly in the process of taking in information from its environment and the ether as signs, archetypes, and imagery and translating it into holograms. It operates predominantly out of radionics where whatever frequency its tuned to, is acts as a receiver for various forms of information within that same frequency that comes in as an acoustic wave that serves to form an electromagnetic field (EMF) as a holographic shape that's composed initially of subtle energy, which provides the blueprint or spatial mapping for constructing an exact replica as its material equivalent. Information inherent in the Ether (Akasha) always comes as a "pairing" or "wave coupling" (like the double helix) that contains both an acoustic sound and optical (visual) image as the geometric patterning inherent in the vibratory frequency.

The two waves of information form an interference pattern that together produce a 3-D holographic image as the subtle template for constructing the material body through a growth and development process. This holographic image as an invisible energy field organises and animates matter into what's called the "phantom effect". This phantom is an invisible 3-D shape as a field formed out of information as a dynamic series of interrelated planes or parallel interlaced and correlating dimensions that operate without any cross-talk to form a chain-of-association as phase conjugation adaptive resonance. When one wave (Monad) resonates with another of the same or similar frequency, they're absorbed into each other forming an interference pattern (Dyad), where certain properties are cancelled out or contradicted, and others are matched and amplified. This adaptation process reformulates the initial generic form (archetype) into a unique variation as the coupling's offspring or combination. This reformulation of internal properties to form a new whole comes by way of what we call "natural selection" as the interaction of complementary opposites that either activate or inactivate each other.

When studying DNA from a purely material perspective of constructing proteins out of encoded genetic information as the selection of qualities from each parent, it was determined that only about 2% of our DNA accounted for this process and the other 98% was what they called "junk DNA", which simply meant they didn't know what it was used for. We now know that the other 98% actually serves as a form of memory bank where information is both written or encoded, and read or decoded, to form a virtual reality out of the information as the pattern or configuration inherent in the vibratory frequency. This works in much the same way the Akashic field of Esoteric Sciences works, where information is contained within the astral plane as archetypal ideas that serve as a generic prototype for creating in the physical realm and are accessed and absorbed into the mind through sympathetic resonance. Within this same astral plane is also stored "thoughtforms" produced by humans as emotional memories that exist as a holographic template that's "recorded" on the Ether (the Akashic book of Life), and not only forms the memory of our soul and body, but also populates the Astral plane of what we call "the Collective Unconscious", or mass consciousness with virtual memories. Our

DNA as a crystalline transmitter and receiver, draws in (resonates with) the thought-forms of others (group mind) as well as ideas from the higher dimension of the mental plane of Universal archetypes, where both come as the holographic information that ultimately serves to program our DNA.

DNA operates by the same principles as the mind and brain, where the acoustic aspect of information as "words" acts to form a visual holographic image in the imagination that turns the idea inherent in the words into a virtual reality. It translates ideas that are communicated by talking about them, whether through our own thoughts as internal dialogue, or as listening to someone else talk, into visual imagery as living scenarios. It comes as words, sentences, paragraphs, and pages of written and spoken script that forms visual imagery in our mind's eye as we read it (absorb it). DNA works by way of the same principles as the mind and neurons of the brain and body. It decodes words into 3-D realities as the basis for organising matter into the biological form that corresponds to the image as an archetypal idea. This is represented in Sacred Geometry by the Tetrad (Tetragrammaton), which is the physical outward reflection and projection of the Triad (inner imagining) that emerges naturally out of the Dyad, which symbolises an interference pattern as the coupling of two waveforms (double helix) of the same frequency to produce a new whole through coherence. Most spiritual texts describe God as the creator calling forth all material life using words as breath that moves across the water (liquid crystal), causing a form to rise up and take shape.

While the genetic make-up of our body doesn't change very much throughout our lifetime, our inner constitution as our character and mental paradigm (vibratory structure) can often change quite drastically. As our inner constitution changes, how we see and what we see in the outer world changes simultaneously. This is because the inner and the outer act as two waveforms that resonate with each other forming an interference pattern that activates different aspects while deactivating others, changing how it's configured. We only see in everything else what's of the same nature (frequency) as we are. As we grow, develop into higher states, and transform mentally and emotionally, how things appear to us changes accordingly. You know when you've undergone transformation of some form by the fact that you begin seeing others and the world in general in a different way. What we notice and how we interpret things to give them meaning changes as an outer reflection of our inner state.

DNA, like the mind, is a fluid-like substance that's always being re-informed by an energetic exchange of subtle energy with everything else around it that's of a similar vibration causing it to constantly flux and morph. It's like a shimmering lustre morphing moment by moment based on what new information or qualities it's absorbing from the environment that modifies its state. Words carried on a certain frequency are naturally inducted into the individual mind where they form an internal image as the reality indicated by the words. Whenever our mind is in a passive and receptive state, such as meditation and hypnosis (Theta-Alpha state), where there's no editing or resistance from the conscious mind (outer awareness), ideas are readily taken in as suggestion, allowed to rise up in the imagination and take hold, and entire realties as an experience are constructed out of them. These holographic realities create a form of inner experience that acts directly on the subconscious mind as the body's consciousness (DNA), to program it through virtual memories.

Matter as particles held together by an invisible electromagnetic field is what forms the primary substance of what we call reality. Matter itself doesn't "possess or generate" consciousness of its own, but acts as the passive receptor for consciousness as vibratory information that structures it into a holistic biological living system. DNA acts as the subtle antenna and receiver for acoustic information that forms a holographic image as an electromagnetic field that provides the blueprint as the etheric body used to construct the physical body. Form and properties always indicate function and how a system operates and behaves. Whenever we change the information used to structure and operate a system, we change how the system forms, expresses, and functions as a whole. The genetic code of our DNA isn't static and fixed, but rather dynamic and always in the process of transforming based on the information as language of some sorts that it acts to absorb, interpret, and shape into an idea.

Scalar energy, as subtle energy, readily moves through and into matter and divides forming an electromagnetic field that serves to organise astral light as essence (photons) into the holographic reality as one possibility (potential) inherent in the scalar wave. Scalar waves exist as a unified field of subtle energy that exists everywhere as what we call "empty space". This empty space, that's commonly called a quantum vacuum, isn't empty at all, but rather filled with holographic information as archetypes used to form, hold together, and sustain the entire material world. It's the invisible field that organises matter into organic and inorganic biological systems that are composed of both an active (animate) and passive (inanimate) aspects.

What this shows us is that our DNA as our subconscious mind or body consciousness is literally programmed by our own thoughts and internal dialogue that are imagined as realities, and from various forms of media that act as suggestions and become the nature of our thoughts. What we hear outwardly forms a picture of reality inwardly. This inward picture formed out of hearing something someone says, becomes a part of our thoughts and provides a holographic image that imprints the DNA of our body with that information as a form of genetic code. DNA, like the mind itself, has the ability to both write and read genetic information. Most of our thoughts are formed from what we've been taught or heard being said, that we incorporate in a harmonious fashion to form our mental paradigm as a working model for perceiving and interpreting the outer world. Any information sent on radio/microwaves in the form of language and pictures, that we take in and think about, not only becomes a part of our vibratory essence in terms of our thinking and feeling, but also as the programming for the DNA of our molecular structure as a corresponding physical equivalent, or the reality inherent in the thoughts.

As we think through a form of internal dialogue where we're talking to ourselves, or whatever we hear and listen to going on around us that we take in

HERMETIC FOLK

The dark rite Isis awaits change . The prophets of old spoke of reincarnation ,at their child's return . Occupying the spaces where thoughts lack manifestation . On the clearest day she is hidden in the darkest area imaginable ! She's the fabric of all things ! The fabric of your dreams !

<u>Enter through the window of your soul</u>

Transcendence Unveiled *Channelled from cosmic energies, artistry of the multidimensional soul! The journey elevates vibrations, Where harmonies, melodies, and healing chimes resonate.*

Sound Temple Meditation *Embark on a journey to the Tree of Life, Along the cosmic river of the soul stream, Receive cosmic downloads from ancient ancestors, Blessed to venture into the sacred space within our minds' eye.*

States of Openness *Desire to share inner worlds, thoughts, fears, hopes, and dreams, In acceptance without judgement or persecution. Embracing differences, finding comfort in our own strengths, Uniting and freeing ourselves and our brothers and sisters.*

Unity in the Garden of Eden *In the beautiful garden of Eden, where all creations live in harmony, Across dimensions of the human/ God mind, Free from daemons or angels, embracing true unity, Growth together in the garden where all thought forms flourish.*

He Was A Soldier / Sorcerer

In the Hour of Strife *At the crossroads of conflict, when choices converge, Can one discern the path of wrong or right? He stood resolute, a soldier true, Amidst the tempest, steadfast in the night.*

enlighten ,

awaken

and Empower your

soul

and your state of consciousness

Ode to the Unseen *By the tongues of twilight and the whispers of stars, The greatest trick, woven in shadows' veils, unfurls: That the Adversary, in silence bound, Didst convince the cosmos, his visage naught, to behold.*

Invocation of the Veil *From the depths where shadows dance, To the heights where light doth lance, In the space betwixt what's known and mist, Reveal the riddle, the cunning twist:*

The Great Concealment *In the tapestry of dusk's domain, Lies the essence of the ancient bane. With whispers soft and cunning guise, He faded 'neath unknowing eyes.*

Epilogue of Denial *So mote it be, in whispered hush, The world convinced, the silence lush. Yet in realms unseen, where shadows grow, The Adversary's truth, his essence flow.*

Thus Spake the Hidden *The greatest trick that e'er was played, By the Adversary's cunning made, In realms unseen, where shadows swirl, He persists, the enigma unfurl.*

Wisdom For Truth Seekers !

Are things in your life working out for you ?

Symbols of Power *Symbols and signs, woven into the fabric of existence, They shape our lives with intent, guide us through unseen realms. Understanding their power empowers you, To coexist as an observer, reader, and wielder of forces, In the multidimensional tapestry of symbols and signs.*

THE UNIVERSE WANTS YOU TO REMEMBER

WE ARE ALL ONE

Healing / Energy Points

The energy that surrounds and influences our body. Both inside and outside of us, that affects our health, our soul / spirit and ultimately our reality .

MOTHS IN THE LIGHT

In a hidden alcove within an ancient library, cloaked in the shadows of forgotten lore, a solitary figure pored over a weathered manuscript. The pages whispered secrets of the universe, scribed in an arcane tongue that resonated with the echoes of time. This was no ordinary seeker; this was Alaric, a magus of profound wisdom, who sought the ultimate light of understanding.

Alaric's journey had always been one of illumination, akin to the moth's instinctive flight towards the flame. He understood that this light, which drew him inexorably, was both a beacon and a mirror, reflecting his deepest yearnings and innate divinity.

"Just as the moth is drawn to the light," he mused, "so are we drawn to a light in this life."

He pondered the familiar, the known. His daily rituals, incantations, and meditations—all these actions sprang from his current understanding, confined within the boundaries of his knowledge.

"In this life, by doing what we know, only the known can be done," he reflected, tracing a sigil in the air.

But Alaric's insight transcended mere observation. He grasped a deeper truth, one that eluded many. His pursuit of light, of wisdom, was not merely an act of discovery but an act of creation. He realised, with a shudder of awe, that in his relentless quest for enlightenment, he was not just a seeker but a god in his own right.

"For without realising it, we are God," he whispered, his voice barely audible in the cavernous room. "For we supplied the light."

Yet, this epiphany led him to a profound and humbling question: "But who supplied the sun?"

The manuscript before him seemed to shimmer, as if acknowledging his insight. It spoke of the ultimate light, the sun, a symbol of the divine source from which all knowledge and existence emanated. This sun was not just the physical star that warmed the earth, but the transcendent beacon of ultimate truth and creation.

Alaric's mind danced with the realisation that his light, his knowledge, was but a fragment of a greater, unfathomable luminescence. The sun was the divine essence, the cosmic force that fueled all existence. He, like all seekers, was but a reflection of this grand illumination, a manifestation of the divine striving towards its own source.

At that moment, Alaric understood his place in the cosmic order. He was both creator and created, a divine spark seeking reunion with the infinite blaze. The path of light he followed was a journey inward and outward, converging at the nexus of the known and the unknown, the finite and the infinite.

With a serene smile, Alaric closed the manuscript, its secrets now etched into his soul. He rose, stepping into the dim light of the li-

brary, knowing that his quest would continue. The path was endless, but each step brought him closer to the heart of the cosmos, where all light converges and all truths are revealed.

Thus, in the grand dance of numbers and stars, of light and shadow, Alaric's journey mirrored the eternal quest of all who seek the divine within and beyond.

The Essence of Resistance

Resistance, in its essence, is not just opposition but the very force that propels life forward. Imagine the universe as a vast dance where everything, from particles to galaxies, flickers in and out of existence at incredible speed—this is the quantum realm. It operates on a fundamental binary principle, akin to the digital world's 0s and 1s, where existence blinks into being and fades away again.

At the heart of this cosmic ballet is Planck's constant (h), a tiny but profound number that signifies the smallest possible unit of energy in quantum mechanics. It represents boundless potential, an eternal wellspring of energy. However, within the confines of time and space, this energy is constrained by Ohm's law, which dictates how energy interacts and flows through systems.

The quantum realm is where unlimited energy manifests momentarily, shaping the universe through its continuous cycles of creation and dissolution. Each moment is both a cause and an effect—a result of the subtle resistance inherent in the fabric of reality. Without this resistance, the dance of existence could not repeat, and the universe as we know it would cease to exist—a concept echoed in the laws of thermodynamics.

This resistance, integral to the quantum's nature, persists through every iteration, influencing the forms and patterns that emerge—from the smallest atomic structures to the grandest cosmic events. It binds all aspects of reality together in a cohesive whole, where each individual, consciously or not, contributes to the ongoing creation and evolution of the universe.

THE FLOWER OF LIFE

This sacred ancient geometric form is the energetic flower bed of which all creations arise. She has been found upon ancient temples and monuments since time immemorial ! It is astonishing that her wisdom and power isn't taught in the mainstream education system as she holds the Keys to the kingdom and yet there lies the very reason why she is not ! Her power and beauty to behold is only found by those that enlighten themselves as to her existence

.

SHE IS THE ENERGETIC FLOWER BED UPON WHICH ALL CRE-ATIONS ARISE

THE HEXAGRAM
IN SACRED GEOMETRY AND SYMBOLOGY
The hexagram is a symbol consisting two equilateral triangles one upwards facing and one inverted , This can be believed to represent the above ethereal/cosmic/macrocosm/energetic realm and the below material/physical/microcosm reality this is shown in the pictures .Its shape and form is intrinsically rooted in the fabric of reality as seen in the stars and the atoms , flowers and so much more . The triangle is a very powerful magic shape as it's the first form / creation neurologically . The hexagram lies on a 6 dimensional axis (see metatrons cube in healing practices) .

The two overlapping triangles create a hexagon at its heart . It is said that King Solomon used this in magic rituals to remove and trap demons and entities . Many cultures and religions around the world have adopted this symbol for the powerful energy it holds which can be harnessed . The hexagram is an immensely powerful sigil that is formed from the flower of life (see above),

Its use in magic rituals can take on infinite forms and strategies

.

AS ABOVE SO BELOW
AS THE UNIVERSE SO THE SOUL
AS WITHIN SO WITHOUT
EVERYTHING IS VIBRATION
EVERYTHING IS IN RESONANCE

PLATO - "HARMONY IS A SYMPHONY , AND SYMPHONY IS AN AGREEMENT BUT AN AGREEMENT OF DISAGREEMENTS , WHILE THEY DISAGREE THERE CANNOT BE , YOU CANNOT HARMONISE THAT WHICH DISAGREES"
DIMENSIONS
Gift of Metatron

Imagine a box inside your mind's eye . There is a cube, it is the gateway to the multidimensional reality of which all things are .
All things are present to you .
Eternal , eternity all within the codes of your DNA .
Encoded into your crystalline symbiosis .
The stardusts immortal creation , future , present past .

A fractal Reality of equality from the macrocosm to the microcosm all united at their heart . Sagittarius A , Andromeda Om Mantra , ,Tetragrammaton , the nucleus of the soul ,
THE MASTER KEY
The cube that lies inside your mind's eye , manifests a creation space .

Imagination is formed within your universal vortices . You may sit focused or unfocused , in thought or inane , it's one and the same , the same as the Sun burns within and without of US ..
VISHNU RA I AM

The energy transmission of Vishnu Ra I am can be received from your knowing of and knowledge of . Just by gazing upon the soul the light codes can be received into your dna and enhance your vibratory field upon ascension to higher realms of awareness and consciousness genesis , The higher self reaches out to all dimensions thus sharing existence ! that connection and flow of energy / light , can be channelled across the planet and received by all of the star vessels ! Namaste /

EVERYTHING IS VIBRATION
ATEN (THE SUN)

As the ancient Egyptians believed . We are all the children of Aten . All life has been granted by ITS unconditional Love . We are Within its Domain and just as we have been birthed From eventually we shall all return to her , including higher dimensional gods , disciples, all of creations eventually evolved to gaze upon wonder and in doing so receive the ability to recognize their god and themselves as part of the process ! Pay homage to that connection and remind us of the wondrous system we are part of and present within .

THE EYE / BLACK HOLE IS THE WINDOW TO THE SOUL

RIVER OF SOULS

Conceived / observed through deep meditation . Some may call this the hell realm or chaos . The vibration screams but on a closer connection is neutral not good or bad it just is ! Many report seeing faces and these were gargoyle like morphing in and out of the ether .

MINDFULNESS - . To be present to yourself and your surroundings ,

To be aware of your actions and the consequences of your actions,

To be conscious to what fills your mind and the effects those thoughts have upon your reality .

THIS SYMBOL IN ALCHEMY IS THE PHILOSOPHER'S STONE
The Philosopher's Stone, that mythic alchemical substance of yore, possesses the fabled power to transmute base metals such as mercury into the resplendent gold or silver; it is also known by the arcane titles of "the Tincture" and "the Powder." Alchemists held the fervent belief that this Stone could concoct an elixir of life, be-

stowing upon the adept the boons of rejuvenation and immortality.

For centuries untold, the Philosopher's Stone was the most coveted prize in the alchemical arts. It stood as the quintessential symbol within the mystical lexicon of alchemy, embodying the apex of perfection, divine illumination, and celestial ecstasy. The arduous quest to unearth the Philosopher's Stone was revered as the Magnum Opus, the Great Work.

Upon deeper reflection, we discern that alchemy's essence extends beyond mere physical transmutation. The alchemical process also signifies the sublime art of transforming lower vibrational thoughts and emotions into higher vibrational resonance—an internal alchemy. Herein lies the true Magick: the elevation of the spirit, the refinement of the soul, and the alignment with the divine.

The Power Of The Mind Is Absolute

The Art Of Manifesting Is Acting Upon Impulse Without RESTRICTION to Achieve the Desired Results

Just Another Day in the Life or The STAR-T of a Whole new World

Your mind WILL create your reality ! What you pay your attention to will undoubtedly become your world and what you observe it to be .

WHAT YOU BELIEVE WILL BE

"take from me ! but do not take from me yet ! as you have not decided what you want to take ! and you are ALL SO unaware of what i have to offer ! When you are aware of both sides then shall the whole coin be REVEALED "

All Things Are Thoughts That The Creator Thinks

Everything moves by the power of soul

All things are constantly changing

The past has gone doesn't exist and the future is yet to happen and doesn't exist the present moment goes so quick it has no permanence soon as you say now it's passed We can never touch the present so in which way would it be said to exist

No past present or future only eternity

SACRED SEXUALITY

Contemplate that supreme moment where each sex infuses itself with the other one giving forth and the other eagerly embracing at that moment through the intermingling of the two natures female acquires Male Vigour and the male is relaxed in female Languor This sweet sacramental act we celebrate is shared in secret because if performed openly before impure eyes the ignorant my mock and the divine power manifesting in both sexes Will shy away .

God, the Cosmos, and Man

In the grand symphony of existence, three great beings stand intertwined: God, the cosmos, and Man. The cosmos, a mirror of God's divine image, and Man, a reflection of the cosmos itself. Each, composed of myriad parts, yet transcending the sum of those parts in their majesty.

Man, crafted as a vessel for God's continued expression of order and beauty in the cosmos, possesses a soul, a life force shared with all beings. But uniquely, Man wields the power of mind, allowing contemplation of the cosmos and communion with God. Thus, Man stands as the nexus between spirit and matter, embodying a dual nature.

The human mind, an echo of God's own, is immortal, eternal, and free. Yet the human body, subject to mortality and the laws of destiny governed by celestial bodies, imposes limitations. Hermes audaciously proposes that this dual nature elevates humanity even above the gods—the celestial beings bound within their eternal orbits.

Man, being both spirit and matter, serves as an intermediary, greater than mortal beings and akin to the immortals. He shares in the creative power of God, crafting gods in his own likeness through the power of his mind.

Man, a marvel worthy of reverence, exists not merely to exist but to transcend his human nature and awaken his divine potential. This potential, to know God, fulfils God's greatest desire for humanity.

Atum stands as the primal, the cosmos as the intermediary, and Man as the culmination. Like the cosmos itself, Man is a whole composed of diverse parts, reflecting unity amidst diversity.

The Maker fashioned Man to govern alongside Him. Should Man embrace this role fully, he becomes a conduit of cosmic order.

Man may understand himself and thereby grasp the cosmos, realising he is the image of Atum and the cosmos. Unlike other living beings, Man possesses the mind, granting him communion with the cosmos, the secondary god, and through contemplation, knowledge of Atum, the supreme god.

Man's body shelters his pure mind like a walled garden, ensuring its peace and protection. He bears a dual nature: mortal in body, immortal in intelligence, exalted yet subject to destiny's dominion.

Human beings, unafraid, stand equal or even superior to the gods of heaven. The quest for spirituality unveils the eternal within the transient—a journey from birth to death, a cycle where the old yields to the new, where decay fosters rebirth.

Human birth marks not a beginning but an incarnation, while death merely ends a particular existence, transforming the soul into another state. Death, shedding the worn-out body, liberates the soul.

The journey beyond death judges the soul's purity, deciding its fate. Pure souls ascend to heavenly realms, while ignorant souls return to the material world, reincarnating until enlightened.

An enlightened soul, having recognized its godlike essence during earthly life, transcends limitations at death, communing with God. Having purified itself, it becomes wholly spiritual and divine, a god in its own right

death and immortality

The end of becoming is the beginning of destruction. The end of destruction is the beginning of becoming everything on Earth must be destroyed because without destruction nothing can be created. The new comes out of the old from decay comes renewal.

Through the cycling course of the celestial gods and the power of nature who has her being in the being of atum for man time is a destroyer but for the cosmos it's never turning wheel

These earthly forms that come and go are illusions

How can something be real that never stays the same but these transitory illusionary things arise from the underlying permanent reality birth is not the beginning of life only of an individual's awareness change into another state death only the ending of this awareness.

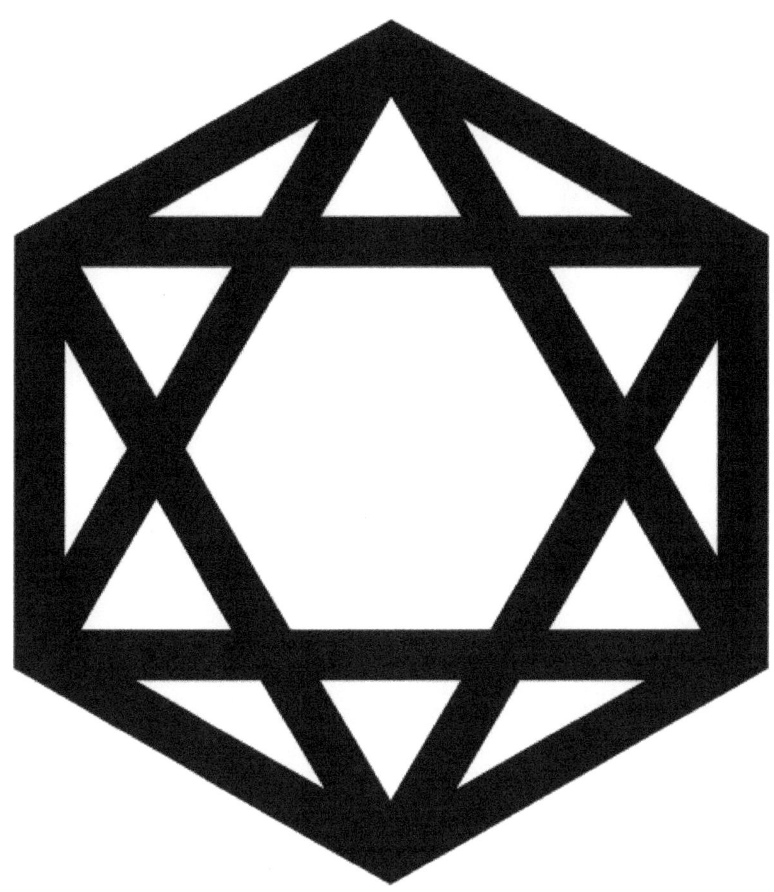

POWER OF 7

The root chakra. The root chakra is the first chakra of the body and is located in the base of the spine. ...

The sacral chakra. ...

The solar plexus chakra. ...

The heart chakra. ...

The throat chakra. ...

The third eye chakra. ...

The crown chakra

The root represents the masculine , the crown the feminine and they are aligned at the heart

7 NOTES TO A MUSICAL SCALE
THAT REPEATS ON THE 8th (INFINITY) NOTE
ALIGNED WITH THE 7 COLOURS OF THE RAINBOW
C Red
D. Orange
E. yellow
F. Green
G. Blue
A. Indigo
B Violet
We will look at this in depth later and see how the whole of existence is aligned

Follow your heart into the world . For the stories of old and new will lead the imagination to undiscovered places, to magic and to revelations.

PERSPECTIVE

FOOD FOR THOUGHT

CHAOS (The Source Of Creation)

Chaos (Ancient Greek: χάος, romanized: kháos) is the mythological void state preceding the creation of the universe (the cosmos) in Greek creation myths. In Christian theology, the same term is used to refer to the gap or the abyss created by the separation of heaven and earth.

According to the Gnostic On the Origin of the World, Chaos was not the first thing to exist. When the nature of the immortal aeons was completed, Sophia desired something like the light which first existed to come into being. Her desire appears as a likeness with incomprehensible greatness that covers the heavenly universe, diminishing its inner darkness while a shadow appears on the outside which causes Chaos to be formed. From Chaos every deity including the Demiurge is born.

The motif of Chaoskampf (German: [ˈkaːɔsˌkampf]; lit. 'struggle against chaos') is ubiquitous in myth and legend, depicting a battle of a culture hero deity with a chaos monster, often in the shape of a serpent or dragon. Parallel concepts appear in the Middle East and North Africa, such as the abstract conflict of ideas in the Egyptian duality of Maat and Isfet or the battle of Horus and Set.

Hesiod and the Pre-Socratics use the Greek term in the context of cosmogony. Hesiod's Chaos has been interpreted as either "the gaping void above the Earth created when Earth and Sky are separated from their primordial unity" or "the gaping space below the Earth on which Earth rests. Passages in Hesiod's Theogony suggest that Chaos was located below Earth but above Tartarus. Primal Chaos was sometimes said to be the true foundation of reality, particularly by philosophers such as Heraclitus.

Chaos has been linked with the term abyss / tohu wa-bohu of Genesis 1:2. The term may refer to a state of non-being prior to creation or to a formless state. In the Book of Genesis, the spirit of God is moving upon the face of the waters, displacing the earlier state of the universe that is likened to a "watery chaos" upon which there is choshek (which translated from the Hebrew is darkness/confusion).

The Septuagint makes no use of χάος in the context of creation, instead using the term for גיא, "cleft, gorge, chasm", in Micah 1:6 and Zacharia 14:4. The Vulgate, however, renders the χάσμα μέγα or "great gulf" between heaven and hell in Luke 16:26 as chaos magnum.

In Hesiod's Theogony, Chaos was the first thing to exist: "at first Chaos came to be" (or was), but next (possibly out of Chaos) came Gaia, Tartarus, and Eros (elsewhere the name Eros is used for a son of Aphrodite). Unambiguously "born" from Chaos were Erebus and Nyx. For Hesiod, Chaos, like Tartarus, though personified enough to have borne children, was also a place, far away, underground and "gloomy," beyond which lived the Titans. And, like the earth, the ocean, and the upper air, it was also capable of being affected by Zeus's thunderbolts.

The notion of temporal infinity was familiar to the Greek mind from remote antiquity in the religious conception of immortality. The main object of the first efforts to explain the world remained the description of its growth, from the beginning. They believed that the world arose out of a primal unity, and that this substance was the permanent base of all its being. Anaximander claims that the origin is apeiron (the unlimited), a divine and perpetual substance less definite than the common elements (water, air, fire, and earth) as they were understood to the early Greek philosophers. Everything is generated from apeiron, and must return there according to necessity. A conception of the nature of the world was that the earth below its surface stretches down indefinitely and has its roots on or above Tartarus, the lower part of the underworld. In a phrase of Xenophanes, "The upper limit of the earth borders on air, near our feet. The lower limit reaches down to the "apeiron" (i.e. the unlimited)."The sources and limits of the earth, the sea, the sky, Tartarus, and all things are located in a great windy-gap, which seems to be infinite, and is a later specification of "chaos"

In Plato's Timaeus, the main work of Platonic cosmology, the concept of chaos finds its equivalent in the Greek expression chôra, which is interpreted, for instance, as shapeless space (chôra) in which material traces (ichnê) of the elements are in disordered motion (Timaeus 53a–b). However, the Platonic chôra is not a variation of the atomistic interpretation of the origin of the world, as is made clear by Plato's statement that the most appropriate definition of the chôra is "a receptacle of all becoming – its wetnurse, as it were" (Timaeus 49a), notabene a receptacle for the creative act of the demiurge, the world-maker.

Aristotle, in the context of his investigation of the concept of space in physics, "problematizes the interpretation of Hesiod's chaos as 'void' or 'place without anything in it'. Aristotle understands chaos as something that exists independently of bodies and without which no perceptible bodies can exist. 'Chaos' is thus brought within the framework of an explicitly physical investigation. It has now outgrown the mythological understanding to a great extent and, in Aristotle's work, serves above all to challenge the atomists who assert the existence of empty space."

Chaos theory is an interdisciplinary scientific theory and branch of mathematics focused on underlying patterns and deterministic laws, of dynamical systems, that are highly sensitive to initial conditions, that were once thought to have completely random states of disorder and irregularities.

Chaos theory states that within the apparent randomness of chaotic complex systems, there are underlying patterns, interconnection, constant feedback loops, repetition, self-similarity, fractals, and self-organisation. The butterfly effect, an underlying principle of chaos, describes how a small change in one state of a deterministic nonlinear system can result in large differences in a later state (meaning that there is sensitive dependence on initial conditions). A metaphor for this behaviour is that a butterfly flapping its wings in Brazil can cause a tornado in Texas.

All notions of order are a myth, the only order of the universe is chaos. Expand your sight and you'll realise, there is order in every chaos.

WORDS CAN ILLUMINATE OR BLIND YOU

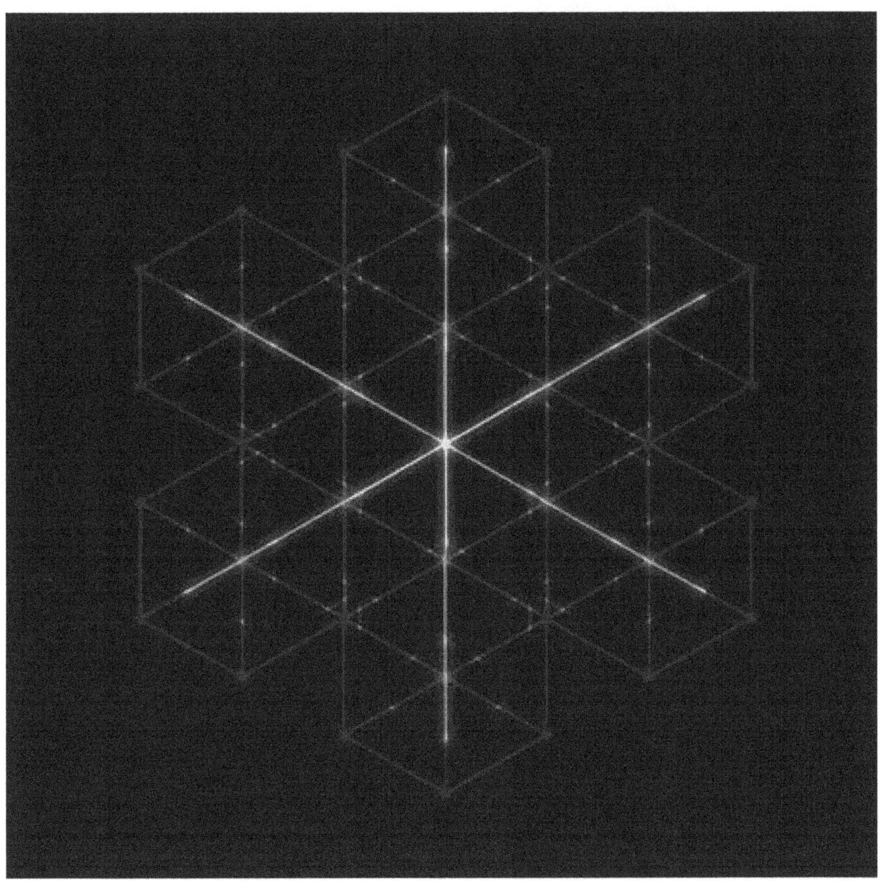

"He who grasps the truth of the Mental Nature of the Universe is well advanced on The Path to Mastery."

— The Kybalion: A Study of the Hermetic Philosophy of Ancient Egypt and Greece.

"I received a telephone call one day at the graduate college at Princeton from Professor Wheeler, in which he said, "Feynman, I know why all electrons have the same charge and the same mass" "Why?" "Because they are all the same electron!". ~ Richard Feynman.

THE ELECTRON

The quantum field/electron has ultimate gravity because it is eternity inside out:

* Eternity inside out is unlimited energy for the least time.

"Eternity is the source of energy." ~ Nikola Tesla.

The universe is the secondary result of quantum recurrence; each repeat the same.

"Take from it as you will, it never runs dry." ~ Tao Te Ching.

Thinking causes the quantum to repeat and this adds virtual resistance to the permanent field.

The introduction of resistance enables time for the universe to exist.

Thus, our thinking produces a virtual universe for the purpose of resolving its own resistance – we go out to gather back while the quantum remains sacrosanct.

"Everything we call real is made of things that cannot be regarded as real." ~ Neils Bohr.

The quantum field was discovered and measured by Max Planck in 1900. He received the Nobel prize but, over the course of time his eternal constant was rearranged to divert from its original thesis.

Truth is truth, we are divine beings.

"The further a society drifts from the truth the more it will hate those who speak it."

~ George Orwell.

AND YOU CAN ALSO COMMIT INJUSTICE BY DOING NOTHING

THE PATH

The path is not one...That is anthropomorphism tree of life...It's not about "genders" only. It's about "form" and "force"...It's about "Beauty" and "the beast"...It's about "white" or "dark"...

You can go down to Malkuth or go up to Kether anyway you want...It doesn't have to be "androgyne"...It's the middle pillar (Buddhist approach -i like Shiva's chaotic approach, there is no goal, you can swirl in it anyway you want-). That's all. Balancing both aspects of your body and mind. Receiver and giver...Strength with compassion...Force with form...Like tai-chi...You move earth (your body) with the will power through water and fire in your veins burning air. As "one entity"...

The Sun Is Older Than The Earth But The Water You Drink is Older Than The Sun

Remember that some of the molecules in your "fresh" sip of water are actually billions of years old—far older than the solar system itself.

It looks doubtful that water existed on Earth before the solar system in which it is located. However, a recent peer-reviewed study published in the journal Science supports this.

Astronomers arrived at this conclusion by demonstrating that water in our solar system had to have been produced inside the huge cloud of gas and dust that preceded and was required for the creation of the star known as the Sun. This implies that water existed before the Sun exploded into a star, water that eventually made its way to Earth via "wet rocks" such as asteroids or comets.

Ted Bergin, an astronomy professor at the University of Michigan in Ann Arbor, is one of the study's authors. Looking back 4.6 billion years, he thinks there is "a magnificent narrative to be told."

Tiny particles smaller than the diameter of a human hair were employed to construct the Earth. This is referred to as "dust" by astronomers, who, according to Bergin, are "very imaginative people."

These dust particles would collect so much energy at this distance from the Sun that they would become too hot for water to form as ice on them. According to Bergin, this shows that the Earth was dry when it was created. Now here's an intriguing conundrum: where did the water come from?

Bergin thinks that a broader question must be asked: Where did the water in the cosmos come from? "The cosmos is made of atoms, not water," he claims. As a result, those atoms in the universe linked together through chemistry at some point in time to become water.

Fortunately, astronomers can analyse that chemical using tools on Earth. They can recreate the conditions that lead to the generation of water. This is accomplished through the use of a technology known as isotope fingerprinting.

This is accomplished through the use of a technology known as isotope fingerprinting. The second type is deuterium. These elements live in a more-or-less constant ratio throughout the solar system: there are approximately 100,000 hydrogen atoms for every deuterium atom. Water may contain this much hydrogen and deuterium.

Chemistry, according to Bergin, "tells us that there can be an excess of deuterium under extremely exact conditions." This is known as a "isotopic fingerprint." Deuterium is plentiful on Earth and in comets and asteroids.

The isotopic fingerprint is only observable at very low temperatures, between 10 and 20 degrees above absolute zero (-441 degrees Fahrenheit). As a result, Bergin writes, "we already know one thing: whatever the source of the water was, it was extraordinarily, incredibly cold." This is due to the Earth's deuterium surplus. As a result, we must analyse how stars and planets form and ask, "Where is it that cold?

Temperatures this low are only possible in two places in the huge, violent system where stars first form: the protostar's surrounding cloud of gas and dust, or the accretion disc that is just beginning to form around it. However, there is one more surprise: water is also generated chemically, in a process called ionisation. The researchers found that the disc is unable to drive it by evaluating a thorough model of this chemical occurrence.

According to Bergin, this shows that the disc, as opposed to the cloud of gas and dust, which are the two most likely sources of water, is unable to do so. Given this, water with an isotopic signature could only have originated from gas and dust about a million years before the sun.

However, this begs the question of how this water ended up on Earth. According to Bergin, planets are formed from the same cloud of gas and dust that compresses and bursts into flame to form a star.

The cloud launched rocks into space, where they collided with the subatomic particles that eventually became Earth. They collided with the Earth and fused with it despite the fact that some of them lacked water. More stones were tossed our way from a distance; these pebbles were chilly enough to hold water.

Therefore, Bergin claims, "when the Earth was birthing, these boulders from larger distances provided the water." The seas, the atmosphere, and the lovely world we have today were all produced as a result of the water that had previously been a component of the rocks simply evaporating through volcanoes.

AS ABOVE SO BELOW

AS THE UNIVERSE
SO THE SOUL

Beginning in the time of Hippocrates, the father of modern medicine, there were medical astrologists who classified diseases based on astrological phenomena — using planetary archetypes to determine how to heal various illnesses with herbs that hold the same archetypal energy.

A similar philosophy of healing that married plants and planetary influences surfaced in a parallel way in many Indigenous cultures and in the ancient practice of Ayurveda in India.

Modern reductionist science has been dismissive of astrology — and herbs, for that matter! Yet what if these ancient pioneers were really onto something important — that the correlation between cosmic influences and the plant kingdom is vital to accessing their healing powers?

In the language of the more cosmic herbalists, different plants are "governed" by different planetary influences. And when we discern those connections, we become clear about how to design remedies that rebalance and heal our bodies.

For example, herbs governed by the sun (which since ancient times has been considered a planet in astrology) were seen to improve cardiovascular function, boost the immune system, and assist with anxiety, depression, resilience, and adaptability.

And herbs ruled by the moon (also long considered a planet in astrology) reduce inflammation, enhance intuition, improve digestion, and assist with sleep.

In some subtle and mysterious way, energetic qualities associated with planetary archetypes enhance the ability of plants to heal us.

While that might sound difficult to believe at first, doctors and medicine people have studied, validated, classified, tested, diagnosed, and effectively healed diseases for centuries based on astrological phenomena — using planetary archetypes...

... and made medicinal preparations that harmonise imbalances within the body, mind, and spirit.

... connecting ancestral ways of diagnostics and the spiritual aspects of the natural world with the preparation and usage of herbal medicine.

SACRED COSMIC HEALING SIGILS

A Cosmic Shaman working with the sacred structures of the Universe , Fabrics and Divine Dimensions

To produce your healing sacred designs to hold in your mind's eye that will change your energies and vibration !

The Infinite Potential of Sigils and Symbols

In the labyrinthine corridors of human consciousness, sigils and symbols wield a power both ancient and profound. Far more than mere marks or designs, they encapsulate a realm of meaning and influence that transcends the limits of their physical form. These symbols, whether ancient glyphs etched into stone or modern logos adorning corporate banners, harbour a secret: they contain within them the potential for infinity.

The Essence of Sigils

Sigils are more than just symbols; they are condensed representations of complex ideas, emotions, and intentions. Created through ritual and imbued with purpose, they act as gateways to deeper layers of consciousness. Each stroke, curve, and line carries meaning and intent, charged with the energy of those who create or invoke them. Like keys to hidden realms, sigils unlock doors to the subconscious mind, where thoughts manifest into reality.

Symbols as Vectors of Control

Throughout history, symbols have been used by elite groups and organisations as tools of control and manipulation. From ancient priesthoods inscribing glyphs of power to modern corporations branding their logos into the global psyche, symbols shape perceptions and guide behaviours. They serve as psychological triggers, activating conditioned responses and shaping cultural narratives. In the hands of those who understand their potency, symbols become instruments of influence, steering mass consciousness towards desired outcomes.

The Subtle Art of Manipulation

Elite companies and institutions harness the power of symbols to influence consumer behaviour, political allegiance, and social norms. Logos of multinational corporations, emblazoned on products and advertisements, embed themselves into the collective psyche, invoking desires and aspirations. Through repetition and association, these symbols create subconscious connections, eliciting emotional responses and fostering brand loyalty. Thus, what appears as a simple logo is, in truth, a sophisticated sigil designed to shape thoughts and control actions.

Breaking the Chains of Influence

Awareness of the potency of sigils and symbols grants liberation from their subtle grip. By recognizing the symbols that surround us—whether in advertising, media, or cultural icons—we reclaim our power to choose and discern. Understanding that symbols encode narratives and agendas allows us to decipher their intended messages and question their influence. This awareness becomes a shield against manipulation, enabling us to see beyond the surface and perceive the deeper currents at play.

Empowerment Through Conscious Choice

Armed with knowledge, we transform passive consumption into conscious engagement. We become active participants in our cultural landscape, questioning narratives, and redefining symbols' meanings. By reclaiming our sovereignty over symbols, we dismantle their power to control and reshape our reality. Each act of conscious awareness chips away at the veneer of manipulation, fostering a collective awakening to the true potential of symbols as tools for personal and societal transformation.

The Quest for Truth and Authenticity

In our journey towards liberation, we strive for authenticity and truth. We seek symbols that resonate with our deepest values and aspirations, forging connections that uplift and inspire.

Through mindfulness and discernment, we navigate the labyrinth of symbols with clarity and purpose, embracing those that align with our vision of a harmonious and just world. In this quest, we discover that symbols, when wielded consciously and ethically, become catalysts for unity, creativity, and profound spiritual growth.

Conclusion: Embracing the Infinite Potential

Sigils and symbols are not mere artefacts of culture or commerce; they are vessels of infinite potential. Within their lines and curves lie the stories of humanity's past, the aspirations of its present, and the possibilities of its future. By understanding their power and reclaiming our agency over them, we transcend manipulation and embrace empowerment. We recognize that symbols, imbued with intention and awareness, have the capacity to shape realities and forge pathways to liberation. As we awaken to this truth, we embark on a journey towards authenticity, unity, and the boundless creativity of the human spirit.

Healing energy .Holding magik qualities and cosmic order

HEALING IS AN HONOUR AND A CALLING

Mark of the mountains the mind must conquer and overcome . From the mountains we see all the lands and from the Mind we can learn and acquire the knowledge to understand them .

transmutes positive ions to negative through intentions and will to heal ! its cosmic nature comes direct from the higher dimensional consciousness

SILVER & GOLD

FEMININE & MASCULINE

SPELLS AND INCANTATIONS

VIBRATIONS CREATE MANIFESTATIONS
INTENTIONS MAKE VIBRATIONS
VIBRATIONS CREATE MANIFESTATIONS
POSITIVE INTENTIONS RAISE VIBRATIONS
SPEAK INTO CREATION
The Power of Words and Spells
You can speak three words, and with wise choices and a plan, the words' spelling casts spells. You can alter your reality by speaking—ask a girl to be your wife, say you quit your job, bid farewell and leave your life. Step into the street, declare "I am here to help; please approach me and ask anything," and you will be introduced to many, with life-changing properties. Essentially, I mean communication—words, spells, are manifestations ◇◇◇.

As far as good and bad go: black, white, up, down, love, and fear. All negativity stems from low vibration, thus it exists, charged, and passed on. But for a Hermetic practitioner, you transmute that energy, understand it out of balance, and bring it into an all-encompassing resonance—that is the quantum state! "I am," which can only be all, leads to your immortal soul! This life is a tiny speck in the grand energetic map of all.

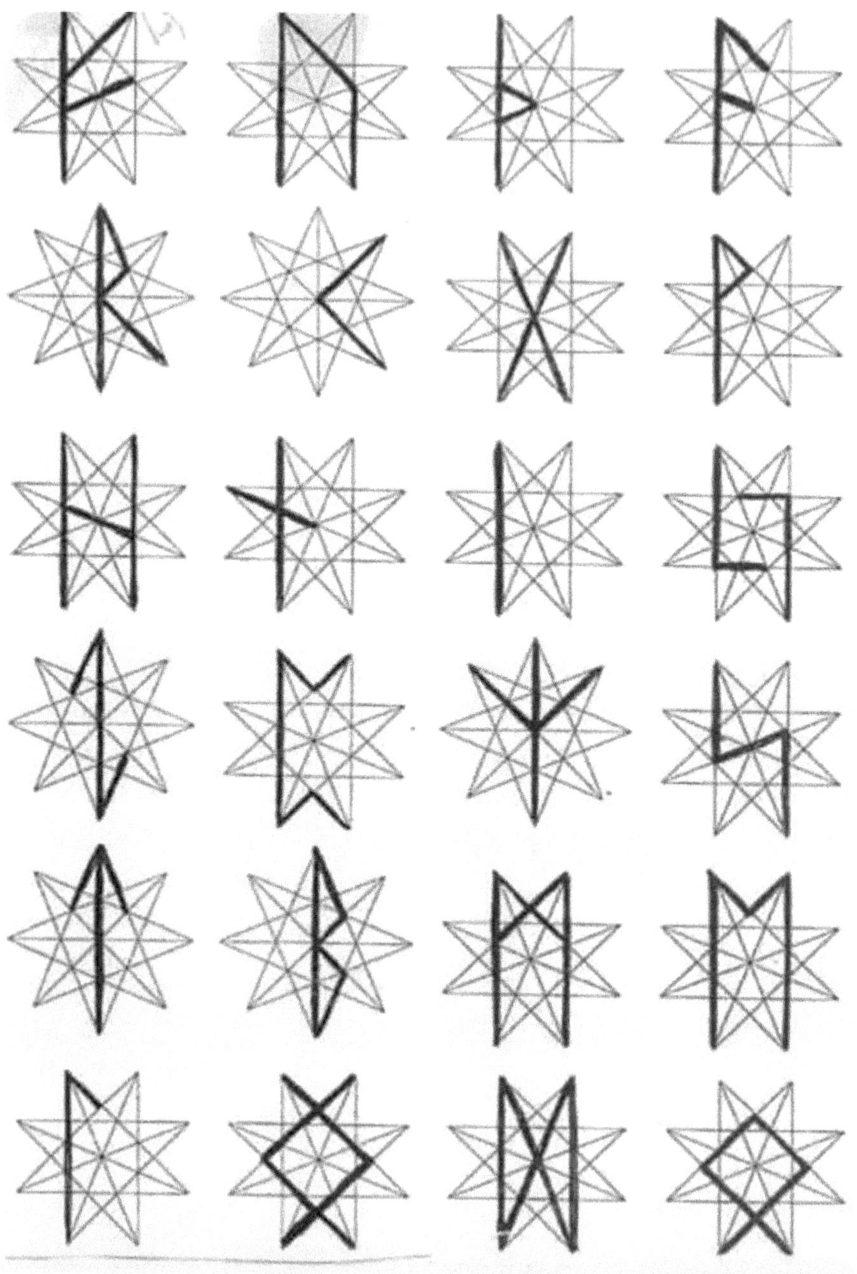

I believe the atoms that make us are Atum, the Creator; each one is connected and, in a sense, are one. It's dimensionally fractal, so by exploring your inner world of self, it's limitless and infinite, as you have been and are all you know—the energetic imprint and peace of a flower!

Deep down, you know how it feels to fly like a bird , to run and hunt as a jaguar . We are of the shamanic/Hermetic consciousness! Fundamentally, it's a belief system—the belief in yourself and the truths and knowledge you uncover and filter. What you believe to be true can come to pass—the power of the mind, body, and soul—mastering your inner energy to alter all things within as without and bringing in a new age to be shared with our children and their children's children . Much love ◈.

WORDS TO WHISPER TO INFINITE VOID

UNTIE ME If I am tied , untie me

when I am lost in the shadows light my way to the path ,

The merciless dance of the sea on the sand gradually taking the earth where we stand ,

If I dissolve solidify me and grant me the knowledge of dissolution ,

Together we stand though apart must become one ,

As the great pyramid ,

We are the rays of light that meet at the sun ,

Energy never dies Everything loops the ouroboros , infinity 0 We are eternal The proof of this.

You are here right now ! only some will understand this. But it is clear to be alive right now isn't a coincidence it's because we exist in the moment.

I always have ,you always will , you are always present ◈ A dream starts with an image and ends with an emotion

"VASHNU RA IAM"

DIVINE UNION

"And then, we are larger than life. For we are angels—the misconception everyone makes about God! That they shall save one or another. By our divine union, we have realised we are here to save ourselves; we are God's will!

I surrender and accept the divine plan, to heal the planet and resonate God-consciousness in divine love, filling our vessels from the soul source. The design is order and chaos and balance. Divine unions producing divine consciousness—understand it and ascend into the Kingdom of Heaven."

THE SECRET

Know the secrets never told, Love, the most perfect word of old. Birthed when you chose to grow bold, Each breath, each beat, a tale untold.

From light or dark, thoughts unfold, In mysteries, your spirit shall be extolled. Through cosmic keys, paths unfold, Tragic truths, the destined mould.

Man, understand and behold, Animals fight, but reach out, be bold. Secrets known to those enrolled, Hidden deep, never to be sold.

Crush anxieties, let them fold, Against their harrowing ploy, be uncontrolled. Know your power, create or mould, Each heartbeat, a magic story told.

Man, rise beyond, be whole, Secrets whispered, let them flow. They'll never learn, let them go, Love, the answer, let it show.

Love, the key, protective flow, Embrace its essence, let it grow.

AT THE END OF THE RAINBOW YOUR FREE

"WHEN WOMEN GIVE THEIR BLOOD BACK TO THE EARTH , MEN WILL COME HOME FROM WAR AND THE EARTH SHALL FIND PEACE " - HOPI PROPHECY

"YOU ARE A RITUAL,

YOUR BREATH IS THE AIR OF KNOWING ,

YOUR BODY GROUNDING EARTH ,

YOUR SPIRIT THE FIRE OF INTENTION ,

YOUR BLOOD THE EBB AND FLOW OF DEEP WATERS EMOTION

YOU ARE A RITUAL ,

NEVER FORGET YOU ARE MAGIC ,

MADE FLESH , BLOOD AND WHOLE ,

AND SACRED SPELLS ARE WRITTEN IN YOUR SOUL"

- CARRIE ARA CAMPBELL

The black oil - beneath the surface of the world realm we find ourselves living in lies, the black oil beneath the Earth beneath the water.

The black oil arose and many use its now to power mechanical creations . It's an alchemical substance, which we use to accelerate our travelling abilities and efficiency purposes just as below us, above us the black oil fills the night sky when the Sun God drops

and reveals the black oil with its geometric star light piercing with formations as we stare out into the night, we can assume we are literally staring into ourselves for beneath our very Feet lies the mirror of the night sky in liquid form, just as liquid cannot be held the black oil flows through your fingertips. You can do your best to contain it, just like a fault, but the power of the black oil is loose, though many believe loose to be weak, but loose has its strengths, just like any degree in polarity! The power of the ocean is immense just as the power of the black oil beneath it is greater from the pressure of the realm above ! Compressed by the reality that it carries ! It is of great potential. Awaiting command and release ! upon staring out into the shadow in the sky We see we are ruled by the geometry of the Earth projected from that space , the creatures and the archetypes in the zodiacs, the beast, the twin, the half man half beast, the lion, the crab, the fish the energy is present in multitudes of dimensional contrast the black oil beneath us responds to your call. It works with the sorcerers will as you call upon the star formation within , it inherently activates the potential the pull in the pool of the black oil like a dragon rising from a fire, just like the moon pulls, the ocean with its presence, the will of the sorcerer commands the geometry to mirror as above, so below the black oil makes it so!

You cannot hold the black oil like any liquid without crafting a cup / a chalice ! These are not natural artefacts but creations from the mind's eye of the creator ! for it flows in ways that will elude you the cup that you craft will only hold the smallest of amounts, but at the full ocean below is required for the results we wish off therefore you must learn to craft the cup Within, but in such amounts a cup will not deliver as the tides go in all directions. Multidimensionally ! So it is so , therefore you must command the energy and hold it without holding it. The power of the black oil is so immense that this should not be undertaken without the greatest and purist of wills ! Of internal cogs , divine wheels ! For any energy put out will return to you with a greater force that's why to achieve the magik you desire. You will eventually learn that you can't have anything ! you will get what serves you best in your growth ! What you need , but if your spirit is one of such high vibration, then your path is not over without struggle as you reap the rewards for your experience in its polarity just like the loose liquid and you will be Kept on course of learning and all of its pitfalls and terrain like your life is a geometrical blueprint, and the journey you Endeavour, is completing it.

The gods of the ancients

Magic in principle

Carl Young said in the Redbook that the key to understanding magic was within the hallucinations you experience in your own mind, so I either through dreams or meditation, or in Hance in the vibration medicines with sacred medicines, I can take that one step further, because understanding your hallucinations will increase your ability to perform, call, execute magical acts tenfold, and not just increases take it to the knowledge of what it is you're actually use it as a tool to enhance your connection to the divine truth from sacred geometry , they are built from the language of the universe by connecting to your hallucinations by connecting to the sight with your minds eye . Within you, structure you create you connect to everything by Tracing a path through the connected universe, you can call a cloud to move back, changing the waves of the ocean, you can cause a plant to grow by calling in the force from the planets above you can calling visitors to your shop, by creating a swirl in the minds of those that are seduced by your stock, and when these faults are put into words and smoking spoken aloud they become even stronger. I just buy fish and I see these connections you will get the results For the fractional universe is all connected.

One hexagon off Metatron's cube is connected to the next and when zooming you find the many , and when you zoom out the many become a few, just like the hexagons of the honeycomb in the hive mother bee called is connected to all And creates the nest the core sense of magic. The singular grain of corn in the sheath in the row in the field in the air will pollinate! I will share with you cause it's been caught ! see ,call it to the understood! This is why we call the common man to its knowledge! Maybe there are hidden texts explaining this which have been withheld and exists only For the few. Eventually, like the corn, it finds a way to reach. The holy grail of knowledge, the blood of Christ and the hidden planes of the occult ! eternal we are !

<u>**GILGAMEK**</u>

The clouds impending collision Was absorbed by Will the closest two edged each other, and the last disappeared dissipated into the ether note. Everything is factual of the one true source of energy/force

Meaning-to affect, you must understand its origin, and what will affect it

I.e./-clouds parted by air, air, controlled by wind/tides, oceans, controlled by moon/force to create an event inside/outside, butterfly, effect, infinite copies of all things

Universies/multi- verses, dimensions, quantum dissolution, and ending the eye/one/source Infinite copies

Galaxies/with blackhole sensors, infinite copies

Suns/with planets surrounding infinite copies

Atoms with proton/neutron electrons surrounding infinite copies.

Intern, making all things we see and a vibration and force fractionalising itself energy transfer in new. paragraph the trial and error or not error, but the riddle of the sphinx, the secrets of the universe light in the Sphinx is here

Saif Al Jabber the very meaning of this word, and the answering of it connects us to the roots of the Sphinx for this planet/star lies in ratio two, where the sphinx lies from the three pyramids, this lies in position from the three stars of Orion's Belt, it's a blue supergiant blue the star traveller pharaoh, cosmic eternal bane

Higher vibration

Connecting you to the quantum mind, and re-source one. The being is all possibilities where the light shines brightest in the iron chamber vibrational healer.

FISKI

The many tools acquired from foreign lands shower, Graton, the bounty of a Fisker, the net, the web cast to the sea to the land, Hler Jord

For Home Dorf harbour set no ledges of the lands. Will the bounty be great, so do an equip ye soul from myrkr where they come to pass of a Fiski leads to celestial skools . Where the physical vessels not pass but harbour the angler of the Kosmos.

All while the chain of anchor must stay Servant un age by decay assistant in freeing the vessel to reap the returns of the fearless Voyager or suffer at the Anki. Death of life of change of dimension, drained of its source of its light of its Anki and thus with movement, comes Hope and change for a hjol dies and fills a new cycle with life. A dimension is born new of death . death - The allie of birth.

he Paradox of Conscious Existence

In moments when we seem absent, lost in the depths of our inner worlds, is it possible that our essence lingers in a realm of our own creation? When faced with declarations of absence or unconsciousness, could it be that our consciousness is more dynamic and vibrant than ever before?

The state of being deemed "brain dead" by external measures might, in fact, mask a profound inner experience. Conventional definitions of life and consciousness may fail to capture the true nature of our existence. This perspective invites us to reconsider the boundaries of consciousness and the mysteries of the human mind.

UNDERNEATH THE BIG TREE , THE BATTLE IS NEVER WON
ALL THE LITTLE FLOWERS ARE FIGHTING FOR THE SUN ,
JUST ONE SEED , GROWS INTO A TREE
BUT IF ALL THE LITTLE FLOWERS DON'T GET WHAT THEY NEED ,
THEY CANT FEED , THEY CAN'T LIVE

The Hierophant's Parable of Dominion and Strife

Beneath the vast canopy of the Ancient One, the eternal conflict persists; the tender blossoms vie for the sacred rays of Sol. The grand Arboreal Monarch, birthed from a solitary seed, ascends to dominion, casting its shadow far and wide.

Yet, behold the plight of the myriad delicate flora: deprived of nourishment, they languish in shadow, unable to sustain the vital flame within. The Grand Cosmic Dance reveals itself here, the paradox of growth and suppression, creation and entropy.

Key Tenets of the Hierophant's Parable:

1. **Dominion and Subjugation:** The Great Tree symbolises power and authority, casting its influence over all beneath it. Yet, this dominion brings about the subjugation of the lesser entities.

2. **Struggle for Vitality:** The flowers' ceaseless struggle for sunlight mirrors the soul's quest for enlightenment amid adversity. It is a battle not merely for survival, but for the essence of being.

3. **Cycle of Creation:** From a single seed springs forth a mighty force. This echoes the occult principle that from the One comes the Many, and yet the Many must contend with the presence of the One.

4. **Balance and Necessity:** The cosmic balance demands that all beings receive their due sustenance. Deprivation leads to

dissolution, a cessation of life force, emphasizing the need for equilibrium in the cosmic order.

5. **Interdependence of Existence:** The grand tapestry of existence is woven from the interconnected fates of all entities. The flourishing of the few should not eclipse the survival of the many.

Embrace this parable, for it unveils the intricate web of life and power. To navigate the mysteries of the cosmic garden is to seek harmony between dominion and compassion, to understand that true power nurtures as much as it commands. Thus, the adept finds wisdom in the shadows and light beneath the Grand Tree, ever striving for the equilibrium that sustains the sacred dance of existence.

Ancient Guardians of the Depths

For over 400 million years, the apex predators of the world have reigned supreme, their forms largely unchanged through the aeons. Among them, the shark, the octopus, and the crocodile stand as timeless sentinels of their domains, masters of their craft. In their unyielding evolution, they have honed their abilities to perfection, becoming unparalleled hunters in the vast expanse of the oceans, rivers, and seas they call home.

These creatures possess an innate prowess, an instinctual understanding of their environment that surpasses mere adaptation—it is a testament to their survival prowess. With precision and efficiency, they navigate the depths, their senses finely tuned to detect the slightest movement, the faintest scent, heralding the presence of prey from miles away.

Yet, as these ancient predators continue to thrive, humanity finds itself at a crossroads. In our quest for progress, we have become increasingly reliant on external forces, relinquishing our primal instincts in favour of convenience and complacency. We are being weaned off our inherent ability to hunt and gather, ceding control to corporations that dictate our consumption habits and shape our future.

In our pursuit of modernity, we risk severing the ties that bind us to our primal roots, forgetting the skills that once ensure our survival. As we disconnect from the natural world, we become vulnerable, dependent on systems that may falter and fail. The apex predators serve as a stark reminder of the consequences of forsaking our primal instincts—of the dangers that lurk when we stray too far from the path of self-reliance.

But there is hope amidst the shadows of uncertainty. Just as the ancient predators have persisted through the ages, so too can humanity reclaim its inherent strength and resilience. By reconnecting with the wisdom of our ancestors, by embracing the skills that have been passed down through generations, we can forge a new path—one rooted in self-sufficiency and empowerment.

The journey ahead may be daunting, but the echoes of the past guide us forward, urging us to reclaim our place as stewards of the earth. For in the timeless dance of predator and prey, lies the essence of life itself—a reminder of the delicate balance that sustains us all.

Upon gazing at the night sky one cool dark evening , the messages of astral light were abundant.

Projected So our souls .

<u>**I AM ENIGMA WE ARE**</u>

In the depths of the abyss, I do not languish as the inert arm-chair, steadfast yet predictable, until fate's scythe severs the limb, and one tumbles into the void. Nor do I resemble the fragile vase, ensconced upon the shelf, a mere vessel awaiting adornment or the inevitable embrace of dust.

Behold, I am akin to the grand piano, dormant yet potent, awaiting the deft touch of a soul to summon forth celestial harmonies, lifting hearts amidst the shadows of despair or offering passage to realms beyond.

I am not akin to the humble mat, trodden upon and discarded in due course, a relic of utility forsaken. Rather, I may be likened to the verdant plant, nurtured by the hand of fate, its growth an enigmatic dance of vitality, where expectation yields to the mysteries of life's unfolding.

As the radiant light piercing through the veil, I bestow warmth and inspiration upon the soul, only to be eclipsed by the tempest's shroud, leaving behind a yearning for my ethereal return, a testament to the longing born of absence.

Yet, I am more than mere illumination; I am the unforeseen power cut, disrupting the fabric of existence, thrusting one into the maelstrom where reality wavers and shifts, a transient voyage through the tempest's embrace.

For I, in essence, am not a fragment adrift in the sea of mundane existence; I am the enigma, woven into the fabric of existence—a riddle yet untold, awaiting the intrepid soul to decipher its mysteries.

The Fundamental Pattern of Existence: A Philosophical Exploration

The exploration of the fundamental patterns of existence often leads us to intriguing intersections between mathematics, geometry, spirituality, and the natural world. By examining the geometric symbol of the hexagram, the probability of being alive, and various natural phenomena, we uncover a profound interconnectedness that hints at a deeper, universal order. This chapter delves into these connections, revealing how they collectively illuminate the nature of existence.

1. The Hexagram: Symbol of Unity and Balance

The hexagram, also known as the Star of David, is composed of two interlocking equilateral triangles. This symbol, appearing in various cultures and spiritual traditions, represents the union of opposites—heaven and earth, spirit and matter, male and female. The geometric perfection and symmetry of the hexagram make it a powerful emblem of balance and unity.

1.1 **Geometric Structure**

- **Two Triangles:** The upward-pointing triangle symbolises active, masculine, and celestial forces, while the downward-pointing triangle represents passive, feminine, and earthly forces. Together, they create a harmonious balance.

- **Six Points and Central Core:** The six outer points represent completeness, while the intersection of the two triangles forms a central seventh point, symbolising unity and the essence that harmonises the dualities.

1.2 **Symbolic Meanings**

- **Spiritual and Material Unity:** The hexagram embodies the integration of spiritual and material realms, reflecting the harmony between heaven and earth.

- **Balance of Opposites:** It signifies the equilibrium of light and darkness, creation and destruction, and other dualities.

- **Holistic Integration:** The central point emphasises the importance of the inner self or soul, integrating all aspects of existence into a coherent whole.

2. The Recurrence of Seven

The number seven recurs in various contexts, symbolising completeness, balance, and spiritual significance. This recurrence is evident in the optimal conditions for life, musical scales, chakras, and natural phenomena.

2.1 **Optimal Blood pH and Probability of Being Alive**

- **Blood pH:** The human body's optimal blood pH level is 7.4, crucial for vital physiological functions.

- **Probability of Being Alive:** The estimated probability of being alive at this moment is approximately 7.4%. This intriguing proximity to 7 highlights a potential numerical harmony in the conditions necessary for life.

2.2 **Seven Vibrational Levels**

- **Musical Scale:** The diatonic scale consists of seven notes, forming the foundation of musical harmony.

- **Chakras:** In many spiritual traditions, there are seven major chakras, each corresponding to different aspects of physical, emotional, and spiritual well-being.

- **Colours of the Rainbow:** A natural spectrum of light splits into seven distinct colours, representing a natural order and completeness.

3. The Principle of "As Above, So Below"

This Hermetic maxim suggests that the macrocosm (the universe) and the microcosm (individual beings) reflect each other. The hexagram, bridging celestial and terrestrial realms, exemplifies this principle.

3.1 **Macrocosmic Perspective: The Sun**

- The sun, a star at the centre of our solar system, is essential for sustaining life. Its energy drives photosynthesis, weather patterns, and biological rhythms, making it a central figure in the cosmic order.

3.2 **Microcosmic Perspective: Atoms and Particles**

- At the atomic level, particles and waves interact in patterns mirroring larger cosmic structures. The hexagram's geometry can be seen as a fractal representation of these patterns, reflecting the interconnectedness of all scales of existence.

4. Fractal Nature and Waveforms

Fractals are complex patterns that repeat at different scales, illustrating the self-similar nature of the universe.

4.1 **Hexagon and Hexagram**

- **Hexagon:** A hexagon's internal angles sum to 720 degrees. When scaled by 10^{-2}, this becomes 7.2, close to the probability of being alive (7.4%). This numerical proximity suggests a fractal relationship.

- **Waveforms:** The hexagram can symbolise waveforms created by particle interactions. Wave-particle duality in physics suggests that particles exhibit wave-like behaviour, resonating with the hexagram's geometric balance.

5. Numerical Patterns and Symbolic Resonance

The correlation between geometric sums, numerology, and existential probabilities reveals a deeper, interconnected reality.

5.1 **Numerical Breakdown:**

- Geometric angle sums often reduce to 9, symbolising completion. This recurring pattern across different shapes highlights the cyclical and fractal nature of existence.

- The alignment of the hexagon's 720 degrees (7.2) with the probability of being alive (7.4%) underscores a symbolic resonance, suggesting an underlying harmony in the universe.

-

Conclusion

The hexagram, with its geometric precision and symbolic depth, encapsulates the essence of balance, unity, and interconnectedness. The recurrence of the number seven in various contexts—optimal conditions for life, musical scales, chakras, and natural phenomena—reinforces this theme. By exploring these connections, we uncover a profound unity that permeates all aspects of existence.

The principle of "as above, so below," embodied in the hexagram, reflects the fractal nature of the universe, where patterns repeat across different scales, from atomic structures to cosmic phenomena. This exploration highlights the intricate web of relationships that sustain life and reveal the deeper, universal truths governing both the microcosm and the macrocosm.

In this way, the hexagram serves as a powerful symbol of the fundamental patterns of existence, offering a deeper understanding of the harmony and order inherent in the universe. This interconnectedness invites us to contemplate our place within the cosmic order, enriching our appreciation of the unity and balance that define our reality.

The Inward Odyssey: A Groundbreaking Philosophy of Cosmic Exploration

Upon contemplating the night sky, it becomes evident that the distances between galaxies and star systems are virtually insurmountable by conventional means. Given our understanding of time, space, and their illusory nature, I have reached a revolutionary conclusion: the pathway to the furthest reaches of the universe lies inwards rather than outwards.

This radical perspective posits that our journey into the cosmos should be guided and driven by the diverse energies emanating from the stars. The constellations, which embody the elemental forces of Earth, serve as celestial maps, guiding our inner responses and deepening our connection to the infinite within. "As above, so below" is not merely a reflection seen at the water's edge but a profound truth echoing through the annals of ancient wisdom.

Civilizations like the Egyptians, the Aztecs, and the Dogon, along with the mythical creatures of old, accessed knowledge and power through their extra-sensory perception. Their legends and deities, often seen as distant and mythical, become accessible through our inner vision, or third eye, and our heart's intuition. This suggests that our chakras—energy centres within our bodies—are essential guides in this enchanted landscape. Clearing and activating these chakras is imperative, as they hold the key to unlocking a journey inwards that is far vaster than the observable universe above.

This philosophy challenges the conventional paradigm of space exploration, suggesting that the most profound discoveries await us not in distant galaxies but within the depths of our own consciousness. It dares us to explore the inner universe, where the energies of the stars and the wisdom of the ancients converge, offering a path to infinite understanding and connection.

By turning our gaze inward, we embark on a journey that transcends the physical limitations of space travel, opening the door to an expansive realm of self-discovery and universal oneness. This inward odyssey invites us to harness the cosmic energies and ancient knowledge that reside within, leading us to a deeper, more profound exploration of the universe than we ever imagined possible.

I am an enigma— enigmas are we

Each thread is unique, each experience distinct, much like a fingerprint. The thoughts and ideas woven throughout this book are interpretations of the messages the universe has whispered to me. These messages may differ for each individual, but they resonate deeply within my soul, a small reflection of the boundless truths I have felt and the profound evidence I have witnessed.

Consider this book a window into my soul, a glimpse into the dance of the universe as I perceive it. My journey has led me through the corridors of wonder and the realms of imagination, guided by an unseen hand that weaves meaning into the fabric of my life. What you will find here are not absolute truths but personal revelations, a tiny fraction of the cosmic puzzle.

Remember that the truths I have uncovered may not be yours. They are filtered through the lens of my experiences, emotions, and perceptions. They are my way of making sense of the mysterious forces that shape our reality. Yet, within this personal narrative lies a universal connection.

This book is an invitation to explore not only my journey but your own as well. To see the universe through my eyes is to open a door to new perspectives, to question, to wonder, and to seek your own truths.

May you find in these pages a spark that ignites your curiosity, a mirror that reflects your own soul, and a reminder that in the grand scheme of things, we are all interconnected. We are all part of the same cosmic dance, each step uniquely ours, yet moving in harmony with the infinite.

" Our Journey through nature's a beautiful thing . We bring what we are and we are what we bring "

Written by Gregory J Smith

The multidimensional Mind Awakening

www.ingramcontent.com/pod-product-compliance
Lightning Source LLC
LaVergne TN
LVHW051055180726
843512LV00019B/1481